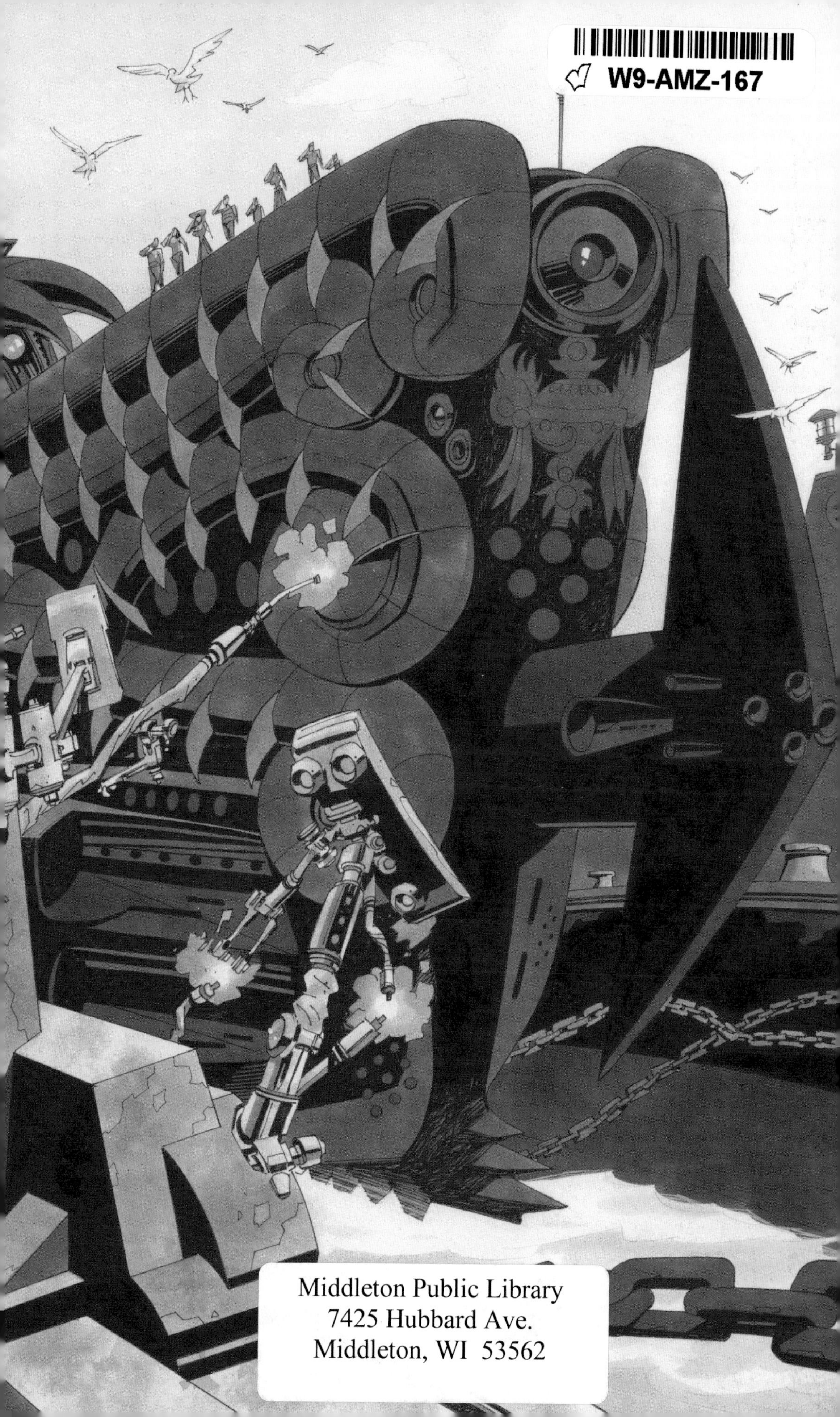

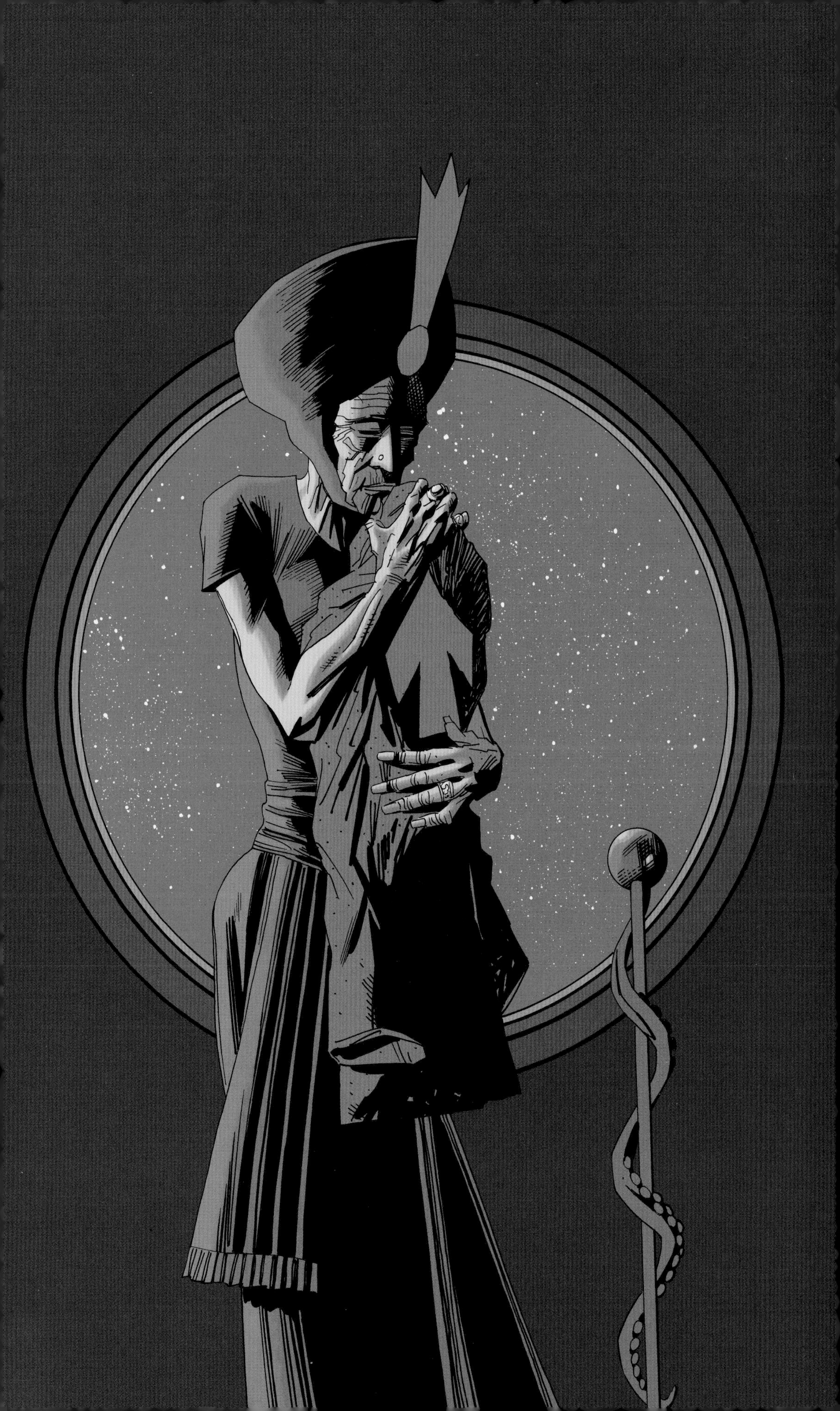

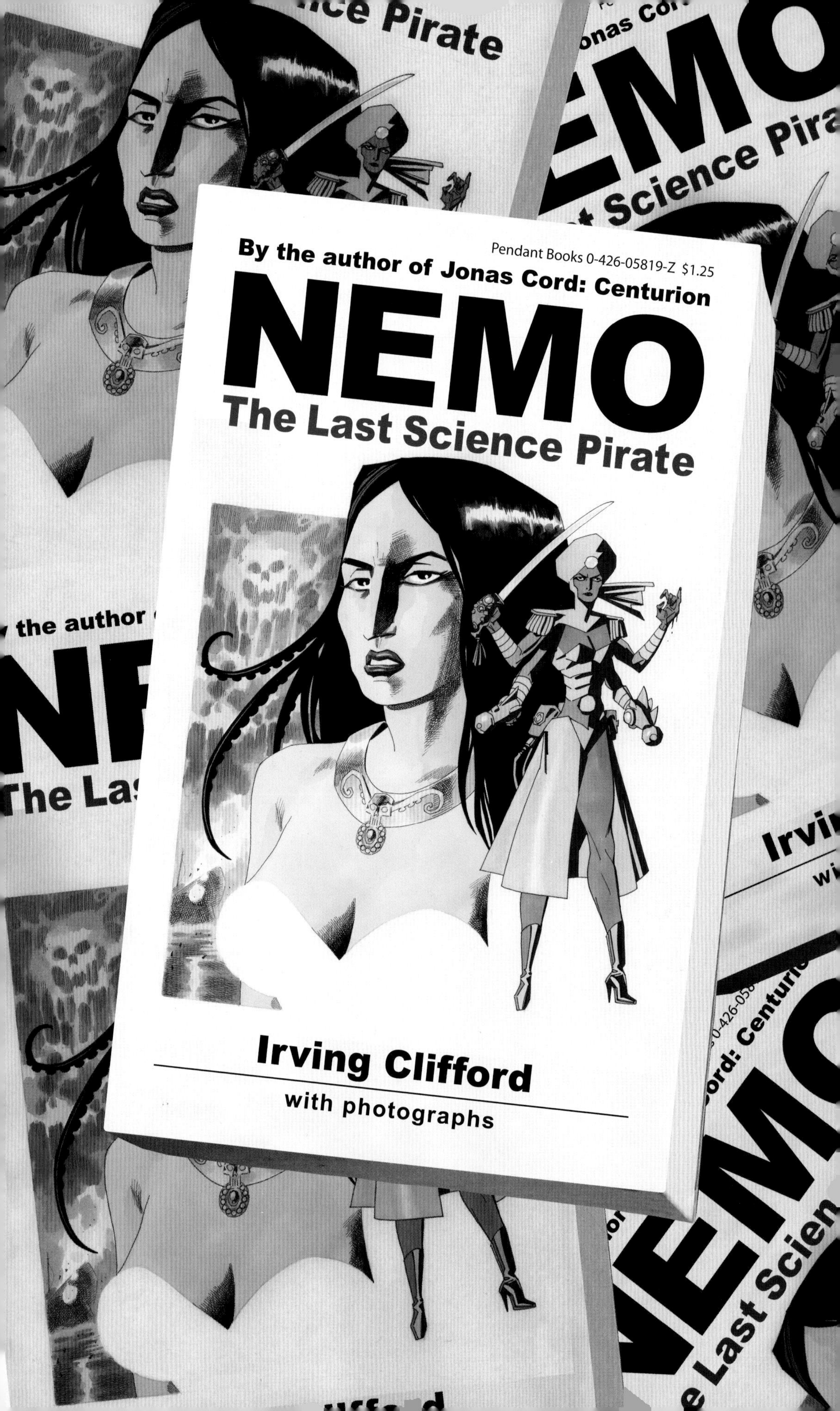

By the author of Jonas Cord: Centurion
Pendant Books 0-426-05819-Z $1.25
NEMO
The Last Science Pirate
Irving Clifford
with photographs

True Sweat FOR MEN

VOL. 18 NO. 4 CONTENTS MARCH, 1975

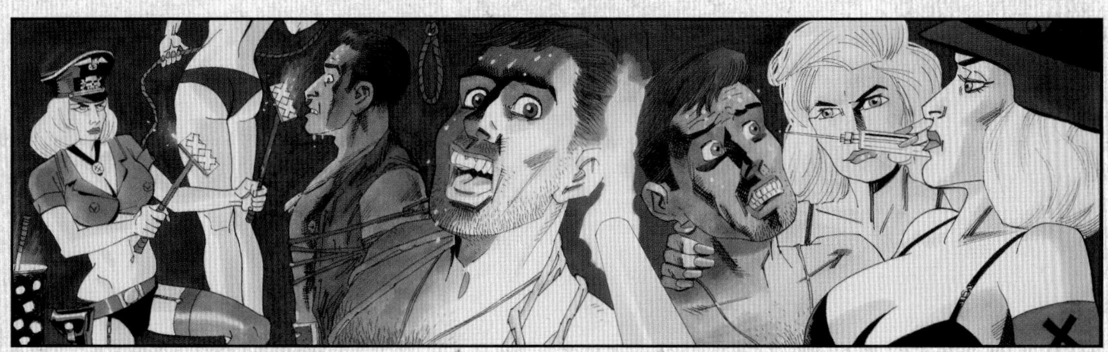

ALL TRUE! ALL SWEAT!

Co-published by Top Shelf Productions, PO Box 1282, Marietta, GA 30061-1282, USA & Knockabout Comics, 42c Lancaster Road, London, W11 1QR, United Kingdom. Top Shelf Productions® and the Top Shelf logo are registered trademarks of Top Shelf Productions, Inc.

First printing, March, 2015. Printed in China.

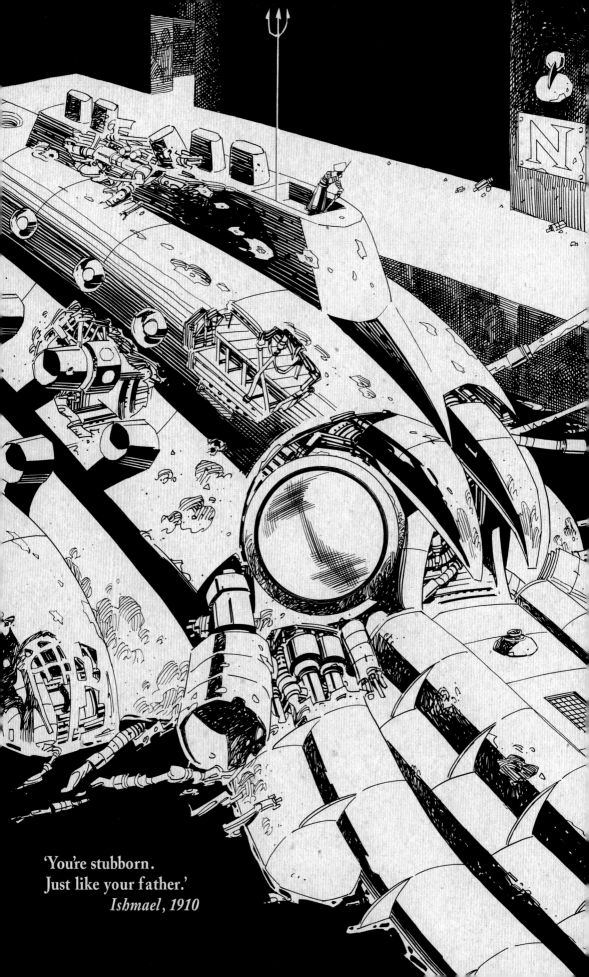

'You're stubborn.
Just like your father.'
Ishmael, 1910

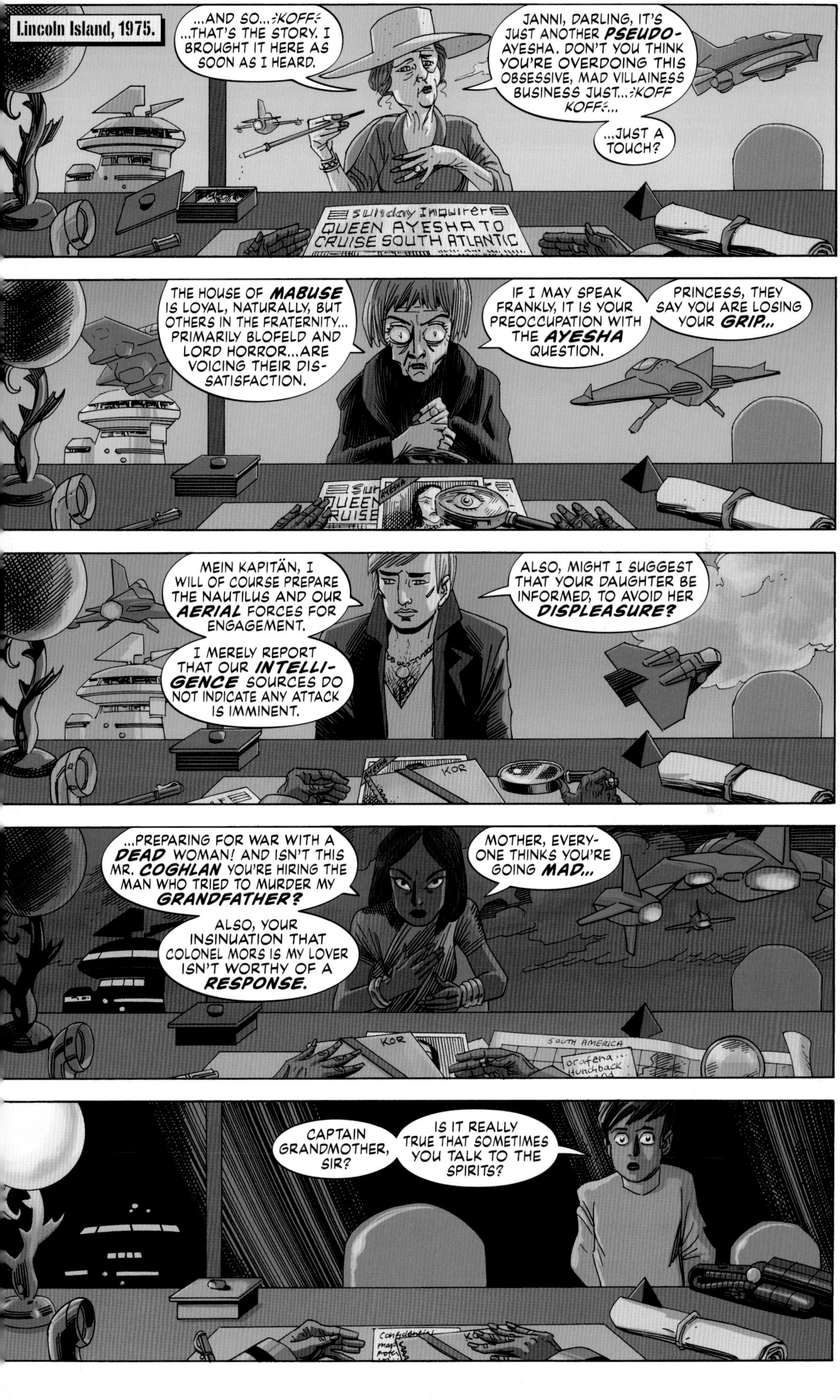
Lincoln Island, 1975.
...AND SO...*KOFF* ...THAT'S THE STORY. I BROUGHT IT HERE AS SOON AS I HEARD.
JANNI, DARLING, IT'S JUST ANOTHER PSEUDO-AYESHA. DON'T YOU THINK YOU'RE OVERDOING THIS OBSESSIVE, MAD VILLAINESS BUSINESS JUST...*KOFF KOFF*...
...JUST A TOUCH?
sunday Inquirer
QUEEN AYESHA TO CRUISE SOUTH ATLANTIC
THE HOUSE OF MABUSE IS LOYAL, NATURALLY, BUT OTHERS IN THE FRATERNITY... PRIMARILY BLOFELD AND LORD HORROR...ARE VOICING THEIR DIS-SATISFACTION.
IF I MAY SPEAK FRANKLY, IT IS YOUR PREOCCUPATION WITH THE AYESHA QUESTION.
PRINCESS, THEY SAY YOU ARE LOSING YOUR GRIP...
MEIN KAPITÄN, I WILL OF COURSE PREPARE THE NAUTILUS AND OUR AERIAL FORCES FOR ENGAGEMENT.
I MERELY REPORT THAT OUR INTELLI-GENCE SOURCES DO NOT INDICATE ANY ATTACK IS IMMINENT.
ALSO, MIGHT I SUGGEST THAT YOUR DAUGHTER BE INFORMED, TO AVOID HER DISPLEASURE?
KOR
...PREPARING FOR WAR WITH A DEAD WOMAN! AND ISN'T THIS MR. COGHLAN YOU'RE HIRING THE MAN WHO TRIED TO MURDER MY GRANDFATHER?
ALSO, YOUR INSINUATION THAT COLONEL MORS IS MY LOVER ISN'T WORTHY OF A RESPONSE.
MOTHER, EVERY-ONE THINKS YOU'RE GOING MAD...
KOR
SOUTH AMERICA
CAPTAIN GRANDMOTHER, SIR?
IS IT REALLY TRUE THAT SOMETIMES YOU TALK TO THE SPIRITS?

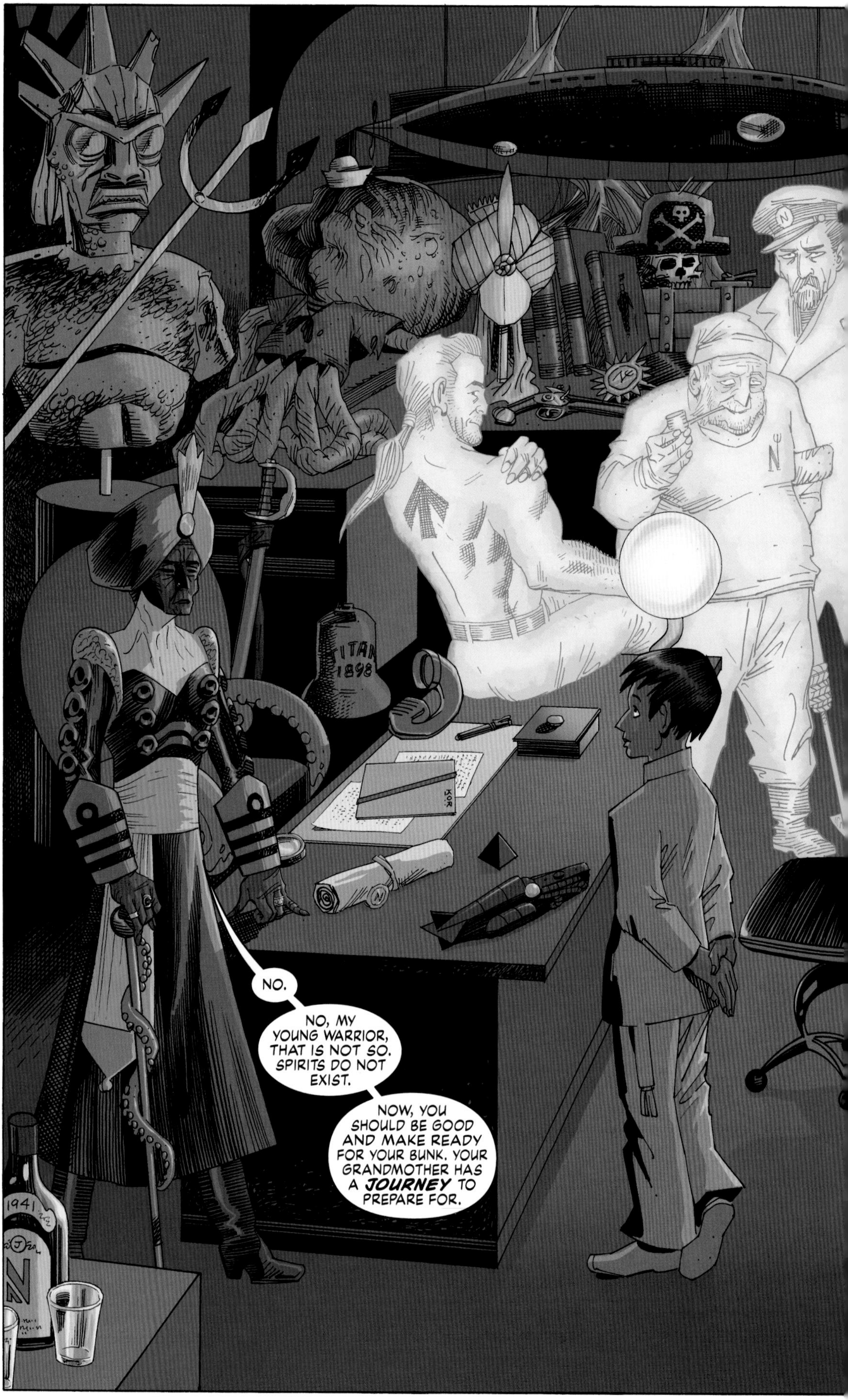
NO.
NO, MY YOUNG WARRIOR, THAT IS NOT SO. SPIRITS DO NOT EXIST.
NOW, YOU SHOULD BE GOOD AND MAKE READY FOR YOUR BUNK. YOUR GRANDMOTHER HAS A JOURNEY TO PREPARE FOR.

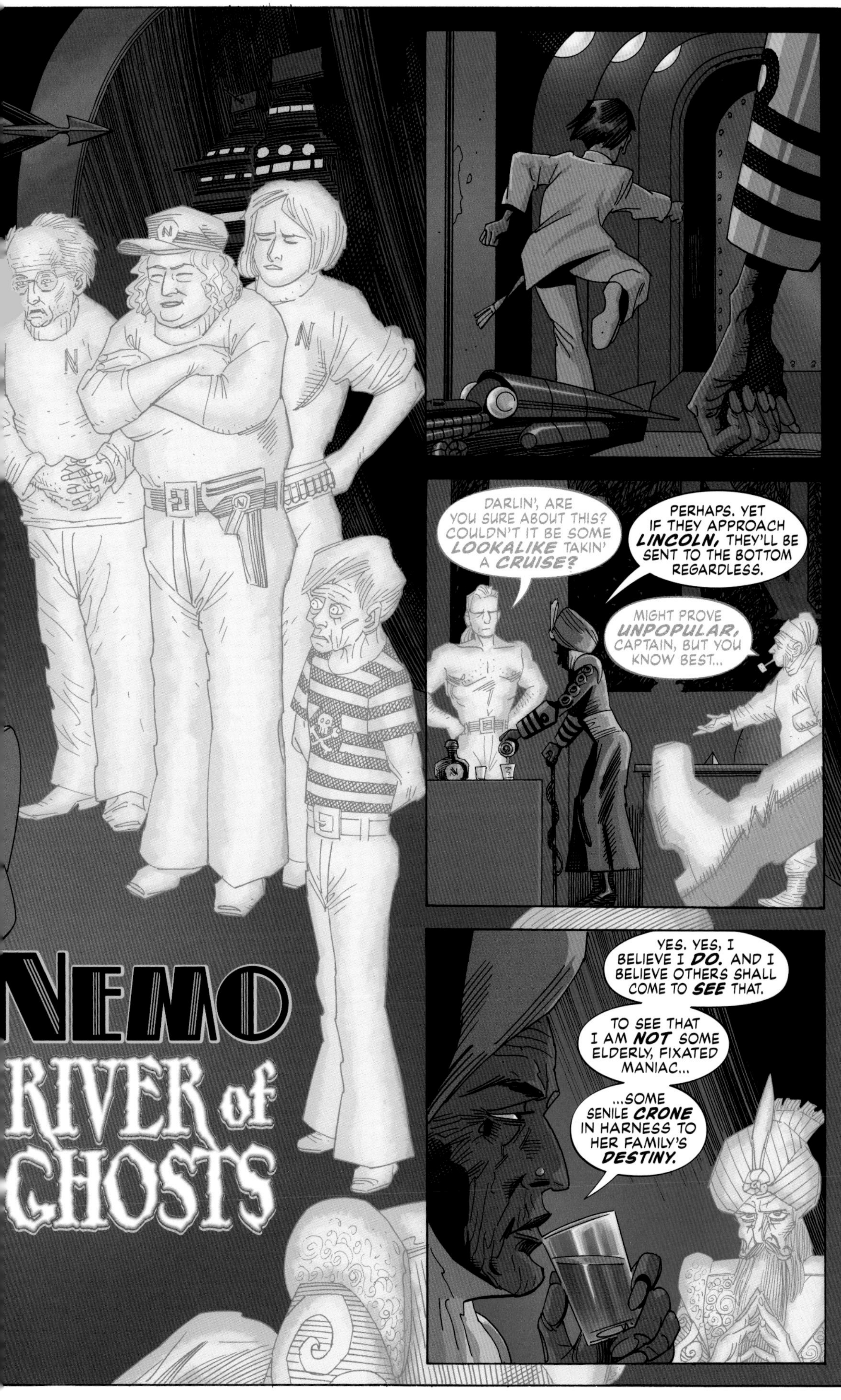
NEMO
RIVER of GHOSTS
DARLIN', ARE YOU SURE ABOUT THIS? COULDN'T IT BE SOME LOOKALIKE TAKIN' A CRUISE?
PERHAPS. YET IF THEY APPROACH LINCOLN, THEY'LL BE SENT TO THE BOTTOM REGARDLESS.
MIGHT PROVE UNPOPULAR, CAPTAIN, BUT YOU KNOW BEST...
YES. YES, I BELIEVE I DO. AND I BELIEVE OTHERS SHALL COME TO SEE THAT.
TO SEE THAT I AM NOT SOME ELDERLY, FIXATED MANIAC...
...SOME SENILE CRONE IN HARNESS TO HER FAMILY'S DESTINY.

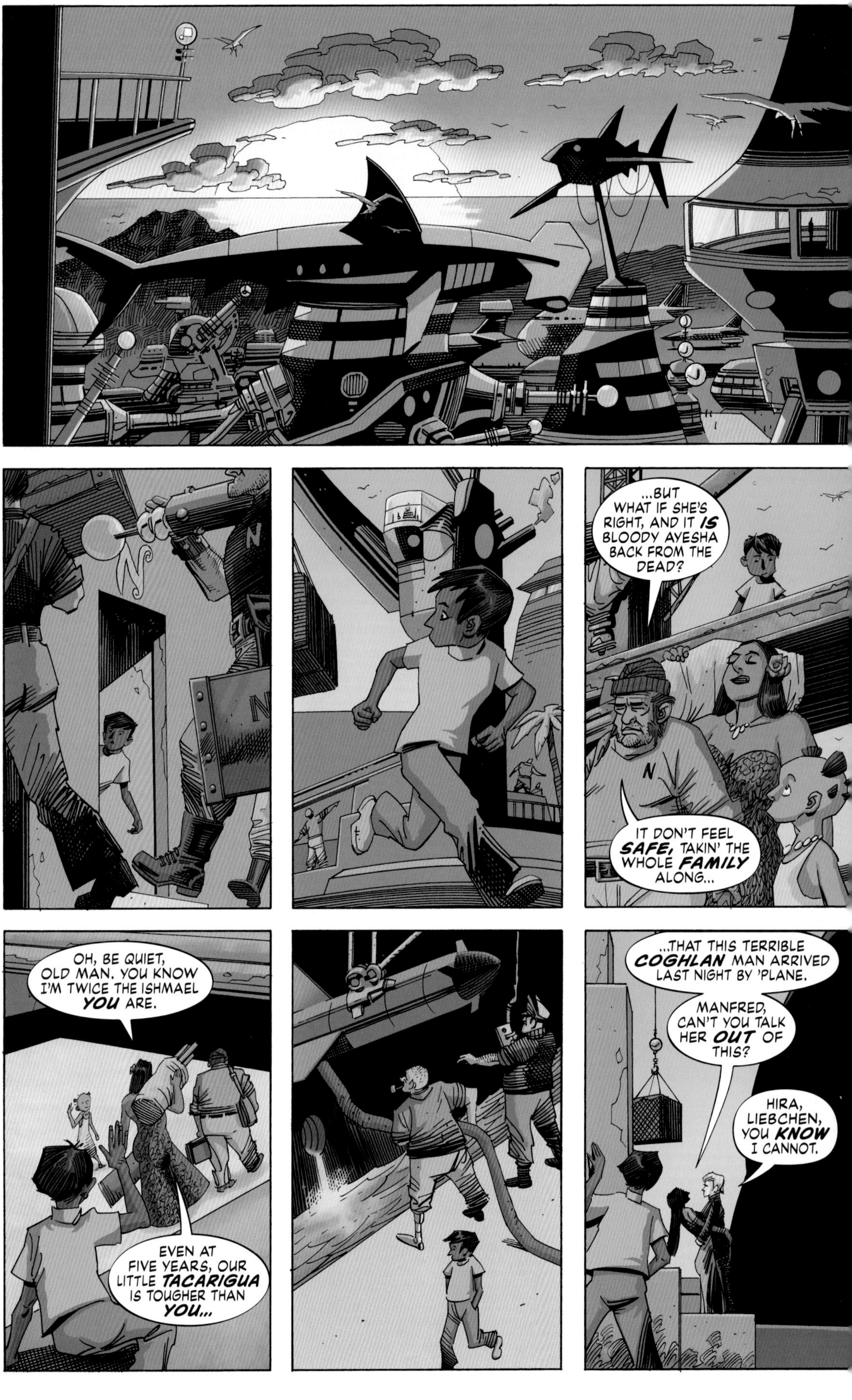

...BUT WHAT IF SHE'S RIGHT, AND IT IS BLOODY AYESHA BACK FROM THE DEAD?
IT DON'T FEEL SAFE, TAKIN' THE WHOLE FAMILY ALONG...
OH, BE QUIET, OLD MAN. YOU KNOW I'M TWICE THE ISHMAEL YOU ARE.
EVEN AT FIVE YEARS, OUR LITTLE TACARIGUA IS TOUGHER THAN YOU...
...THAT THIS TERRIBLE COGHLAN MAN ARRIVED LAST NIGHT BY 'PLANE.
MANFRED, CAN'T YOU TALK HER OUT OF THIS?
HIRA, LIEBCHEN, YOU KNOW I CANNOT.

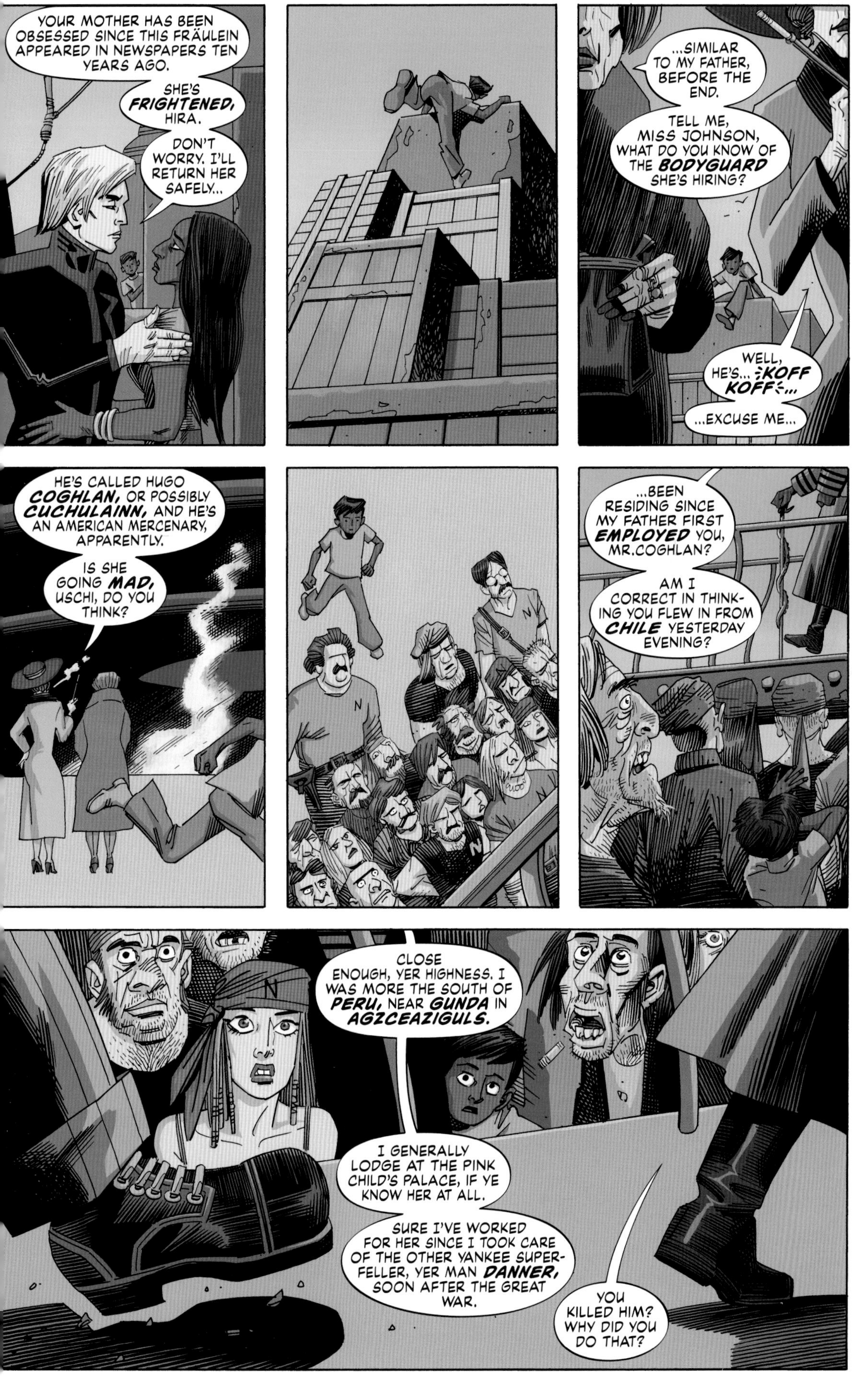
YOUR MOTHER HAS BEEN OBSESSED SINCE THIS FRÄULEIN APPEARED IN NEWSPAPERS TEN YEARS AGO.
SHE'S *FRIGHTENED,* HIRA.
DON'T WORRY. I'LL RETURN HER SAFELY...
...SIMILAR TO MY FATHER, BEFORE THE END.
TELL ME, MISS JOHNSON, WHAT DO YOU KNOW OF THE *BODYGUARD* SHE'S HIRING?
WELL, HE'S... *KOFF KOFF*...
...EXCUSE ME...
HE'S CALLED HUGO *COGHLAN,* OR POSSIBLY *CUCHULAINN,* AND HE'S AN AMERICAN MERCENARY, APPARENTLY.
IS SHE GOING *MAD,* USCHI, DO YOU THINK?
...BEEN RESIDING SINCE MY FATHER FIRST *EMPLOYED* YOU, MR.COGHLAN?
AM I CORRECT IN THINKING YOU FLEW IN FROM *CHILE* YESTERDAY EVENING?
CLOSE ENOUGH, YER HIGHNESS. I WAS MORE THE SOUTH OF *PERU,* NEAR *GUNDA* IN *AGZCEAZIGULS.*
I GENERALLY LODGE AT THE PINK CHILD'S PALACE, IF YE KNOW HER AT ALL.
SURE I'VE WORKED FOR HER SINCE I TOOK CARE OF THE OTHER YANKEE SUPER-FELLER, YER MAN *DANNER,* SOON AFTER THE GREAT WAR.
YOU KILLED HIM? WHY DID YOU DO THAT?

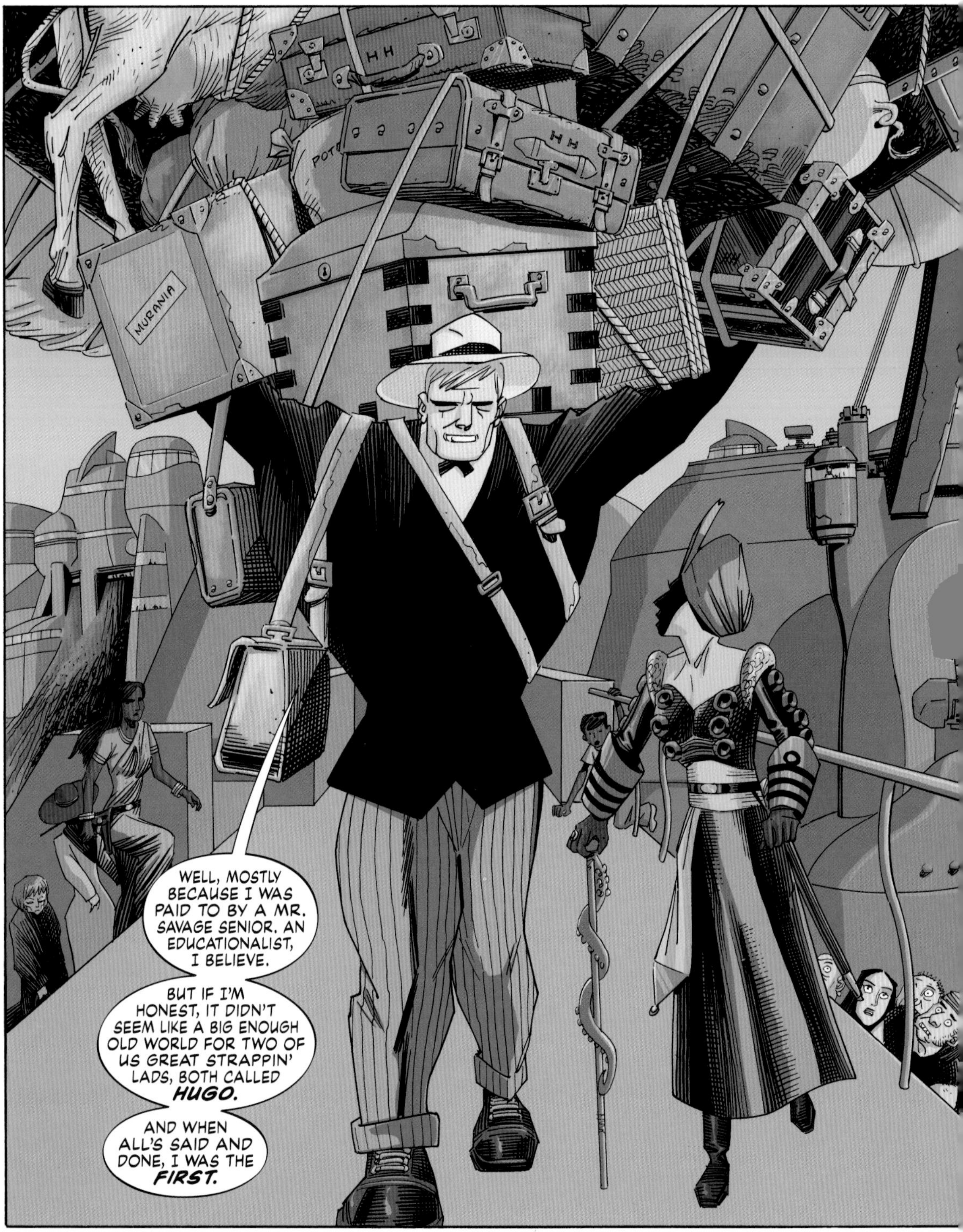
WELL, MOSTLY BECAUSE I WAS PAID TO BY A MR. SAVAGE SENIOR. AN EDUCATIONALIST, I BELIEVE.
BUT IF I'M HONEST, IT DIDN'T SEEM LIKE A BIG ENOUGH OLD WORLD FOR TWO OF US GREAT STRAPPIN' LADS, BOTH CALLED ***HUGO.***
AND WHEN ALL'S SAID AND DONE, I WAS THE ***FIRST.***
MURANIA

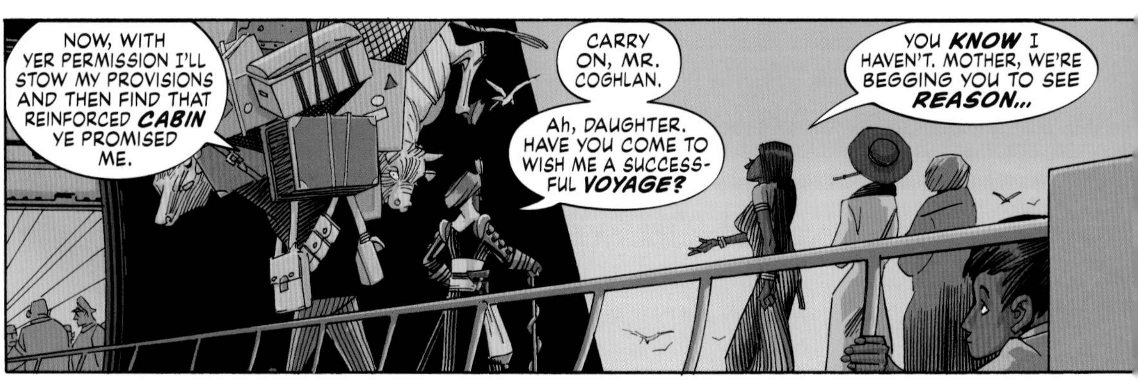
NOW, WITH YER PERMISSION I'LL STOW MY PROVISIONS AND THEN FIND THAT REINFORCED ***CABIN*** YE PROMISED ME.
CARRY ON, MR. COGHLAN.
Ah, DAUGHTER. HAVE YOU COME TO WISH ME A SUCCESSFUL ***VOYAGE?***
YOU ***KNOW*** I HAVEN'T. MOTHER, WE'RE BEGGING YOU TO SEE ***REASON...***

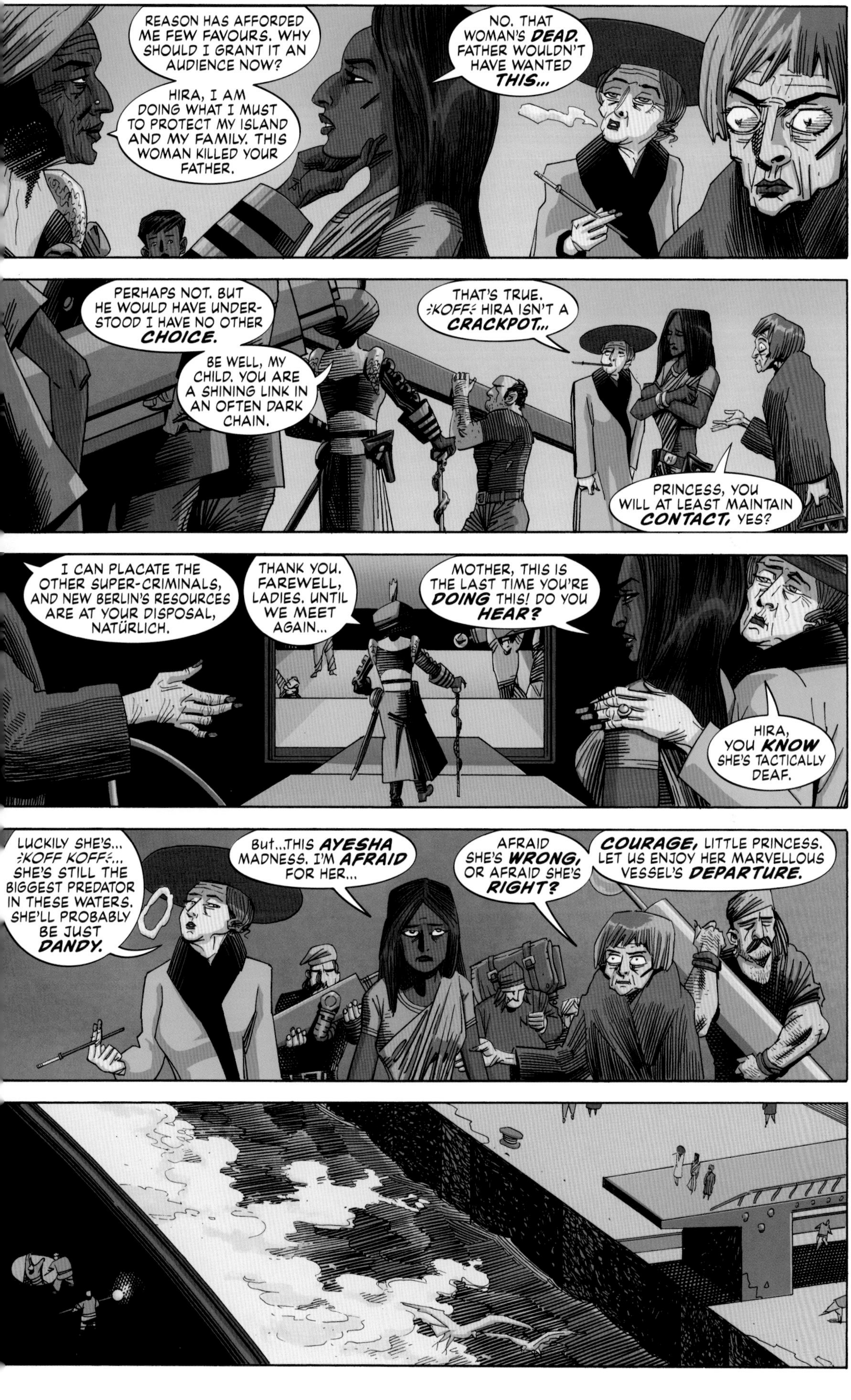

REASON HAS AFFORDED ME FEW FAVOURS. WHY SHOULD I GRANT IT AN AUDIENCE NOW?
HIRA, I AM DOING WHAT I MUST TO PROTECT MY ISLAND AND MY FAMILY. THIS WOMAN KILLED YOUR FATHER.
NO. THAT WOMAN'S DEAD. FATHER WOULDN'T HAVE WANTED THIS...
PERHAPS NOT. BUT HE WOULD HAVE UNDERSTOOD I HAVE NO OTHER CHOICE.
BE WELL, MY CHILD. YOU ARE A SHINING LINK IN AN OFTEN DARK CHAIN.
THAT'S TRUE. KOFF HIRA ISN'T A CRACKPOT...
PRINCESS, YOU WILL AT LEAST MAINTAIN CONTACT, YES?
I CAN PLACATE THE OTHER SUPER-CRIMINALS, AND NEW BERLIN'S RESOURCES ARE AT YOUR DISPOSAL, NATÜRLICH.
THANK YOU. FAREWELL, LADIES. UNTIL WE MEET AGAIN...
MOTHER, THIS IS THE LAST TIME YOU'RE DOING THIS! DO YOU HEAR?
HIRA, YOU KNOW SHE'S TACTICALLY DEAF.
LUCKILY SHE'S... KOFF KOFF... SHE'S STILL THE BIGGEST PREDATOR IN THESE WATERS. SHE'LL PROBABLY BE JUST DANDY.
But...THIS AYESHA MADNESS. I'M AFRAID FOR HER...
AFRAID SHE'S WRONG, OR AFRAID SHE'S RIGHT?
COURAGE, LITTLE PRINCESS. LET US ENJOY HER MARVELLOUS VESSEL'S DEPARTURE.

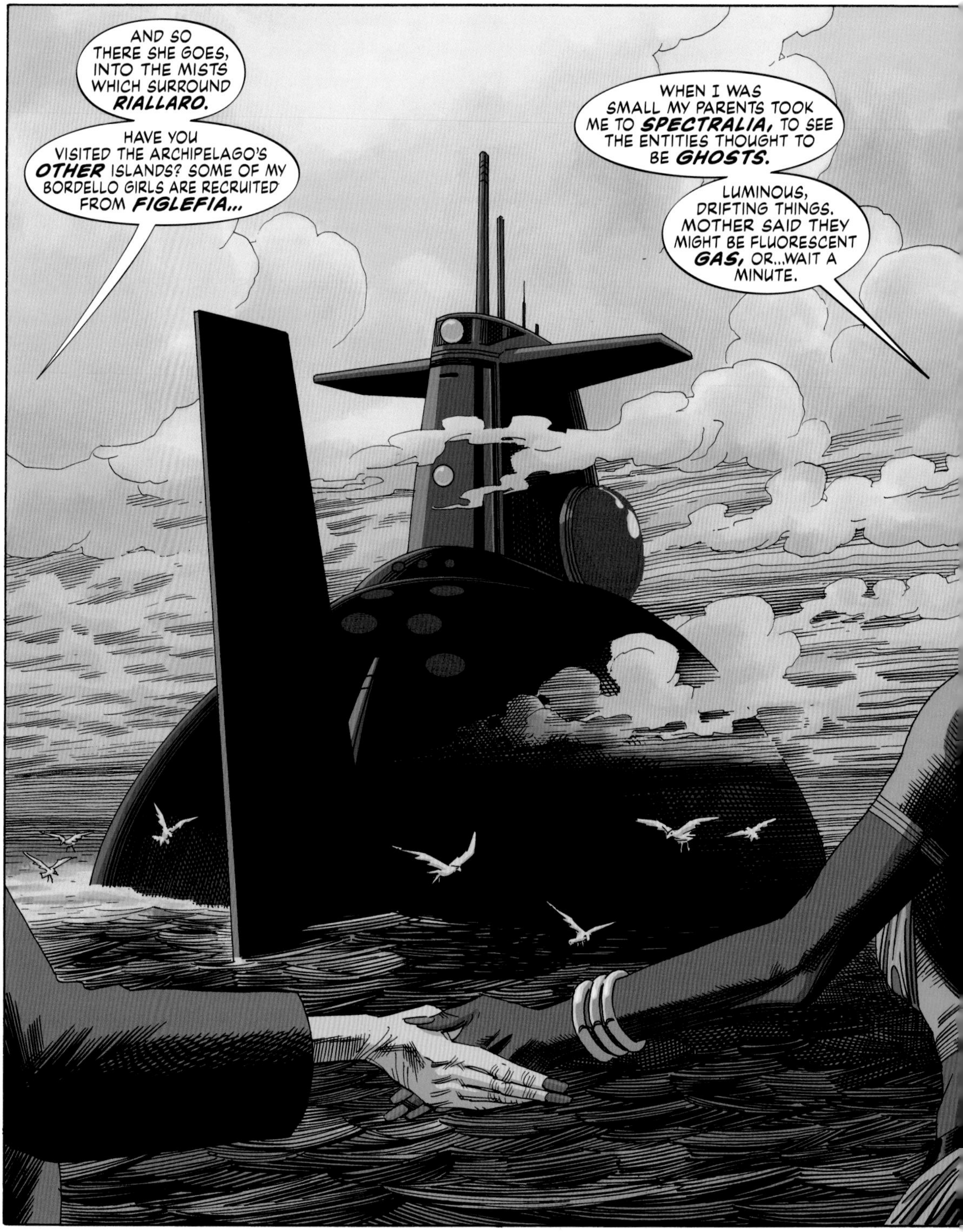
AND SO THERE SHE GOES, INTO THE MISTS WHICH SURROUND RIALLARO.
HAVE YOU VISITED THE ARCHIPELAGO'S OTHER ISLANDS? SOME OF MY BORDELLO GIRLS ARE RECRUITED FROM FIGLEFIA...
WHEN I WAS SMALL MY PARENTS TOOK ME TO SPECTRALIA, TO SEE THE ENTITIES THOUGHT TO BE GHOSTS.
LUMINOUS, DRIFTING THINGS. MOTHER SAID THEY MIGHT BE FLUORESCENT GAS, OR...WAIT A MINUTE.

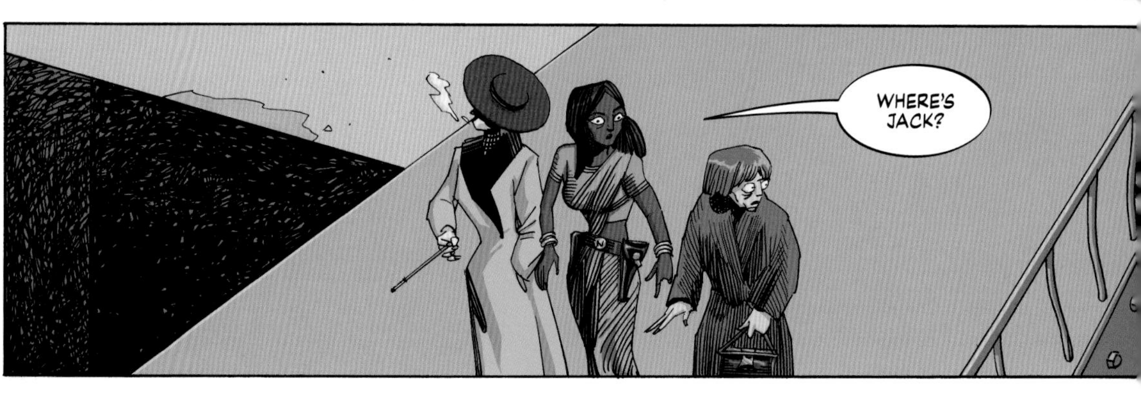
WHERE'S JACK?

THE TORPEDO TUBES?

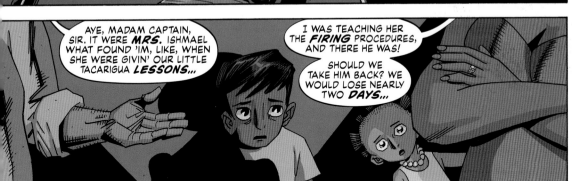

AYE, MADAM CAPTAIN, SIR. IT WERE *MRS.* ISHMAEL WHAT FOUND 'IM, LIKE, WHEN SHE WERE GIVIN' OUR LITTLE TACARIGUA *LESSONS...*

I WAS TEACHING HER THE *FIRING* PROCEDURES, AND THERE HE WAS!

SHOULD WE TAKE HIM BACK? WE WOULD LOSE NEARLY TWO *DAYS...*

TWO *DAYS?* WITH THAT SHE-WOLF ALMOST UPON US? OF *COURSE* NOT.

LISTEN TO ME VERY CAREFULLY. YOU HAVE ENDANGERED THIS MISSION. YOU ARE A DISGRACE TO THE DISCIPLINE OF THIS VESSEL.

AT THE LEAST PROVOCATION, MINNOWS SHALL FEAST UPON YOUR EYES.

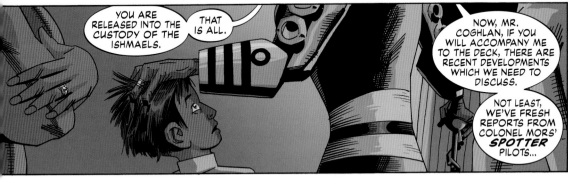

YOU ARE RELEASED INTO THE CUSTODY OF THE ISHMAELS.

THAT IS ALL.

NOW, MR. COGHLAN, IF YOU WILL ACCOMPANY ME TO THE DECK, THERE ARE RECENT DEVELOPMENTS WHICH WE NEED TO DISCUSS.

NOT LEAST, WE'VE FRESH REPORTS FROM COLONEL MORS' *SPOTTER* PILOTS...

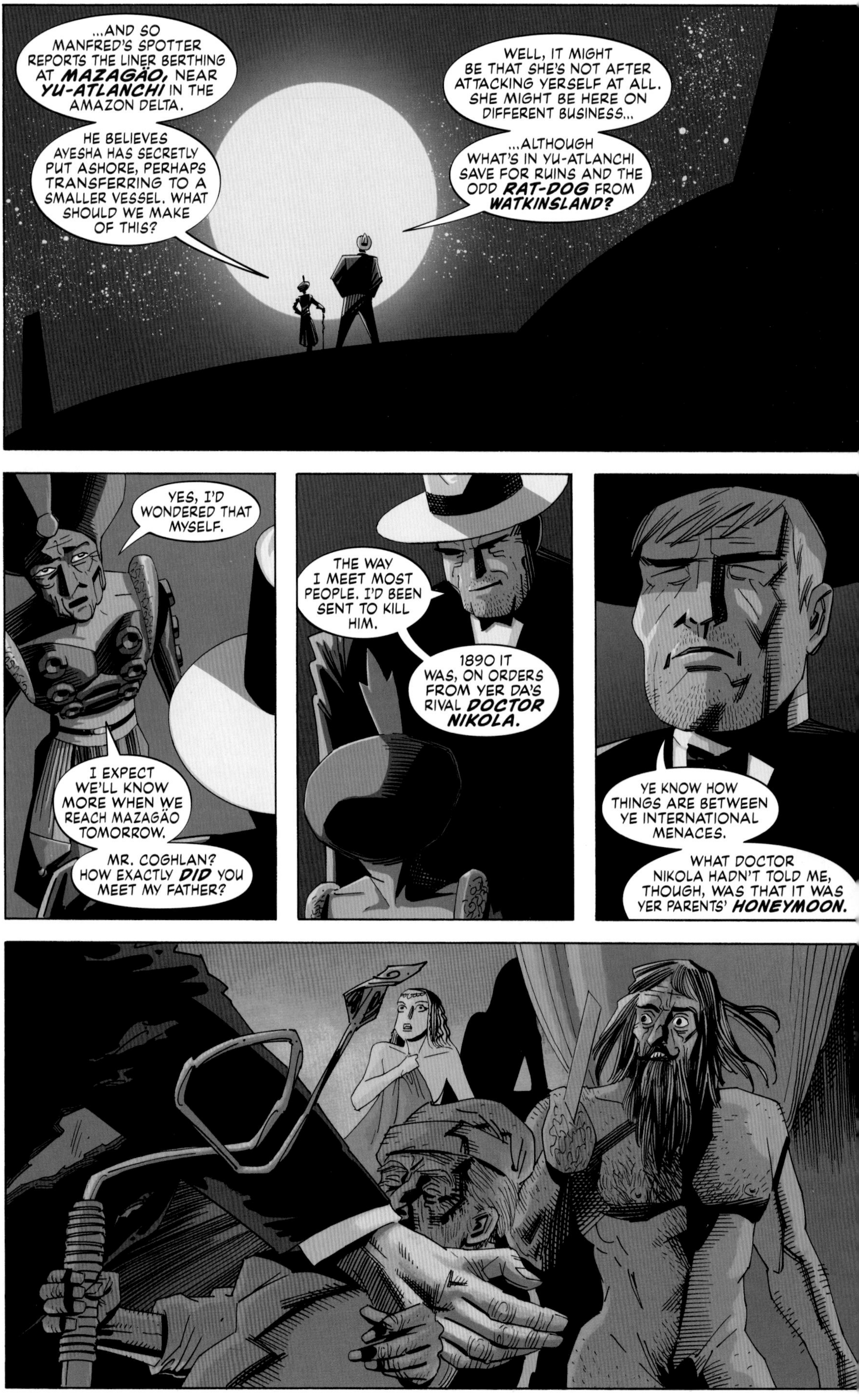
...AND SO MANFRED'S SPOTTER REPORTS THE LINER BERTHING AT MAZAGÃO, NEAR YU-ATLANCHI IN THE AMAZON DELTA.
HE BELIEVES AYESHA HAS SECRETLY PUT ASHORE, PERHAPS TRANSFERRING TO A SMALLER VESSEL. WHAT SHOULD WE MAKE OF THIS?
WELL, IT MIGHT BE THAT SHE'S NOT AFTER ATTACKING YERSELF AT ALL. SHE MIGHT BE HERE ON DIFFERENT BUSINESS...
...ALTHOUGH WHAT'S IN YU-ATLANCHI SAVE FOR RUINS AND THE ODD RAT-DOG FROM WATKINSLAND?
YES, I'D WONDERED THAT MYSELF.
I EXPECT WE'LL KNOW MORE WHEN WE REACH MAZAGÃO TOMORROW.
MR. COGHLAN? HOW EXACTLY DID YOU MEET MY FATHER?
THE WAY I MEET MOST PEOPLE. I'D BEEN SENT TO KILL HIM.
1890 IT WAS, ON ORDERS FROM YER DA'S RIVAL DOCTOR NIKOLA.
YE KNOW HOW THINGS ARE BETWEEN YE INTERNATIONAL MENACES.
WHAT DOCTOR NIKOLA HADN'T TOLD ME, THOUGH, WAS THAT IT WAS YER PARENTS' HONEYMOON.

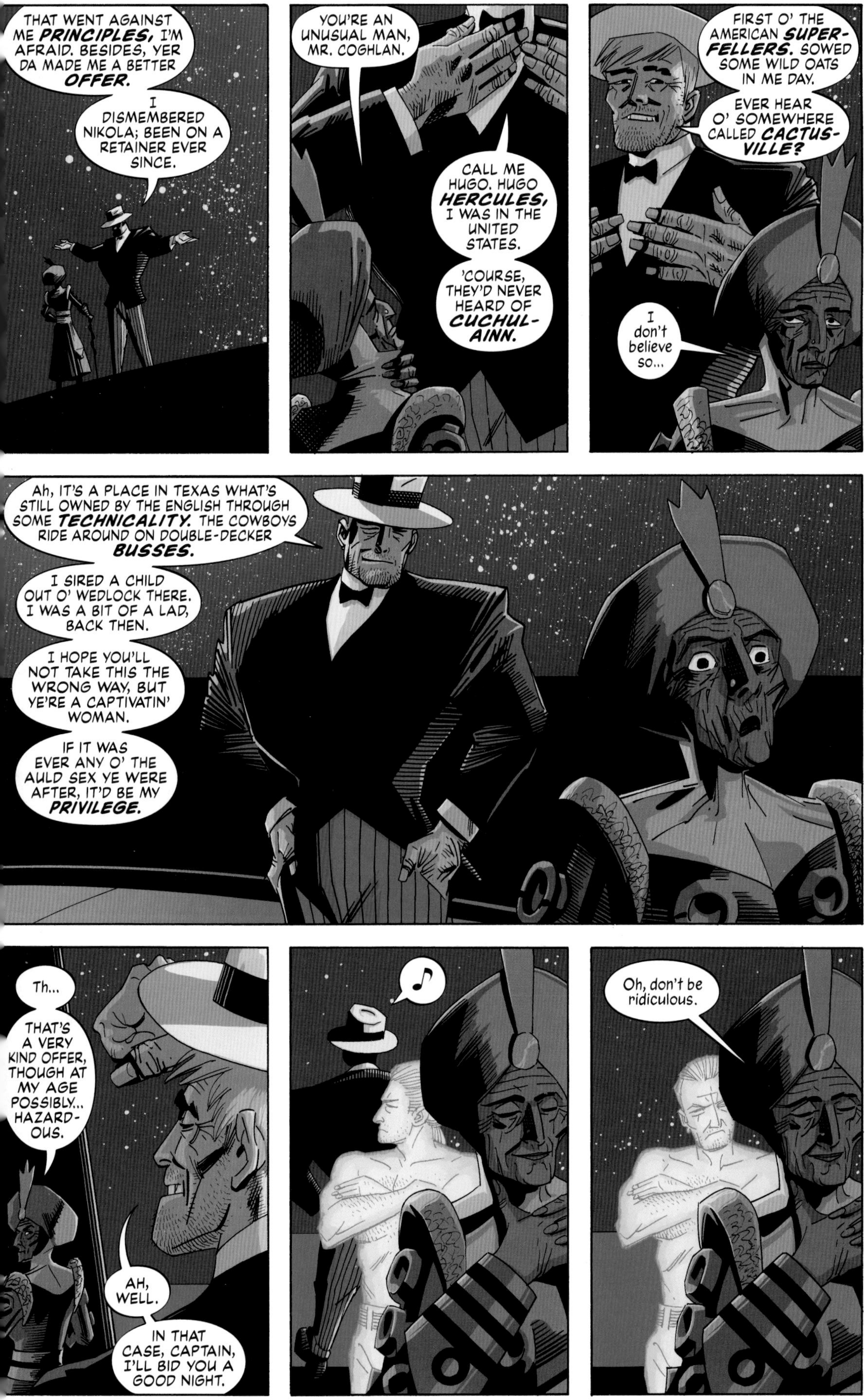
THAT WENT AGAINST ME PRINCIPLES, I'M AFRAID. BESIDES, YER DA MADE ME A BETTER OFFER.
I DISMEMBERED NIKOLA; BEEN ON A RETAINER EVER SINCE.
YOU'RE AN UNUSUAL MAN, MR. COGHLAN.
CALL ME HUGO. HUGO HERCULES, I WAS IN THE UNITED STATES.
'COURSE, THEY'D NEVER HEARD OF CUCHULAINN.
FIRST O' THE AMERICAN SUPER-FELLERS. SOWED SOME WILD OATS IN ME DAY.
EVER HEAR O' SOMEWHERE CALLED CACTUSVILLE?
I don't believe so...
Ah, IT'S A PLACE IN TEXAS WHAT'S STILL OWNED BY THE ENGLISH THROUGH SOME TECHNICALITY. THE COWBOYS RIDE AROUND ON DOUBLE-DECKER BUSSES.
I SIRED A CHILD OUT O' WEDLOCK THERE. I WAS A BIT OF A LAD, BACK THEN.
I HOPE YOU'LL NOT TAKE THIS THE WRONG WAY, BUT YE'RE A CAPTIVATIN' WOMAN.
IF IT WAS EVER ANY O' THE AULD SEX YE WERE AFTER, IT'D BE MY PRIVILEGE.
Th...
THAT'S A VERY KIND OFFER, THOUGH AT MY AGE POSSIBLY... HAZARDOUS.
AH, WELL.
IN THAT CASE, CAPTAIN, I'LL BID YOU A GOOD NIGHT.
♪
Oh, don't be ridiculous.

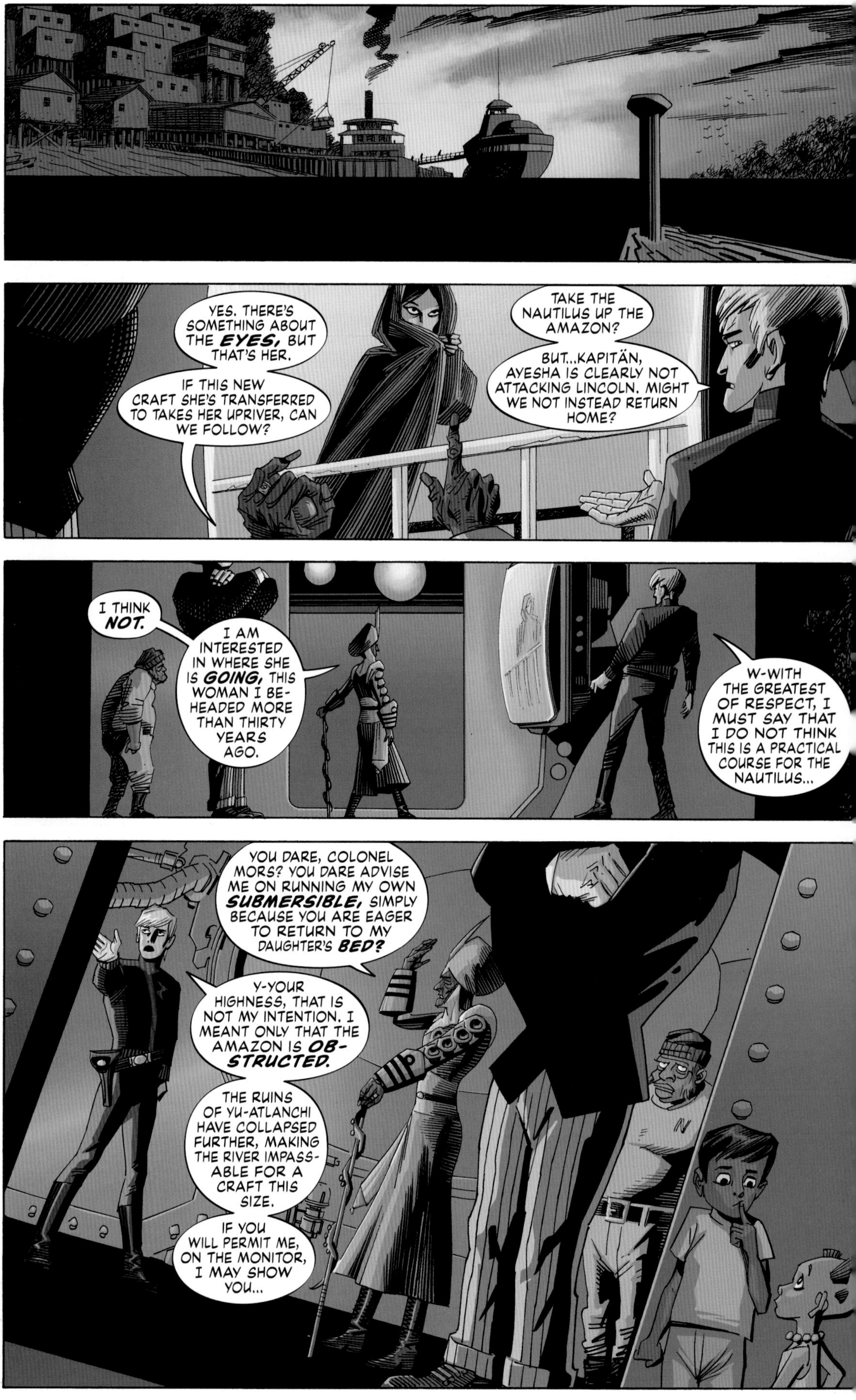
YES. THERE'S SOMETHING ABOUT THE EYES, BUT THAT'S HER.
IF THIS NEW CRAFT SHE'S TRANSFERRED TO TAKES HER UPRIVER, CAN WE FOLLOW?
TAKE THE NAUTILUS UP THE AMAZON?
BUT...KAPITÄN, AYESHA IS CLEARLY NOT ATTACKING LINCOLN. MIGHT WE NOT INSTEAD RETURN HOME?
I THINK NOT.
I AM INTERESTED IN WHERE SHE IS GOING, THIS WOMAN I BE-HEADED MORE THAN THIRTY YEARS AGO.
W-WITH THE GREATEST OF RESPECT, I MUST SAY THAT I DO NOT THINK THIS IS A PRACTICAL COURSE FOR THE NAUTILUS...
YOU DARE, COLONEL MORS? YOU DARE ADVISE ME ON RUNNING MY OWN SUBMERSIBLE, SIMPLY BECAUSE YOU ARE EAGER TO RETURN TO MY DAUGHTER'S BED?
Y-YOUR HIGHNESS, THAT IS NOT MY INTENTION. I MEANT ONLY THAT THE AMAZON IS OB-STRUCTED.
THE RUINS OF YU-ATLANCHI HAVE COLLAPSED FURTHER, MAKING THE RIVER IMPASS-ABLE FOR A CRAFT THIS SIZE.
IF YOU WILL PERMIT ME, ON THE MONITOR, I MAY SHOW YOU...

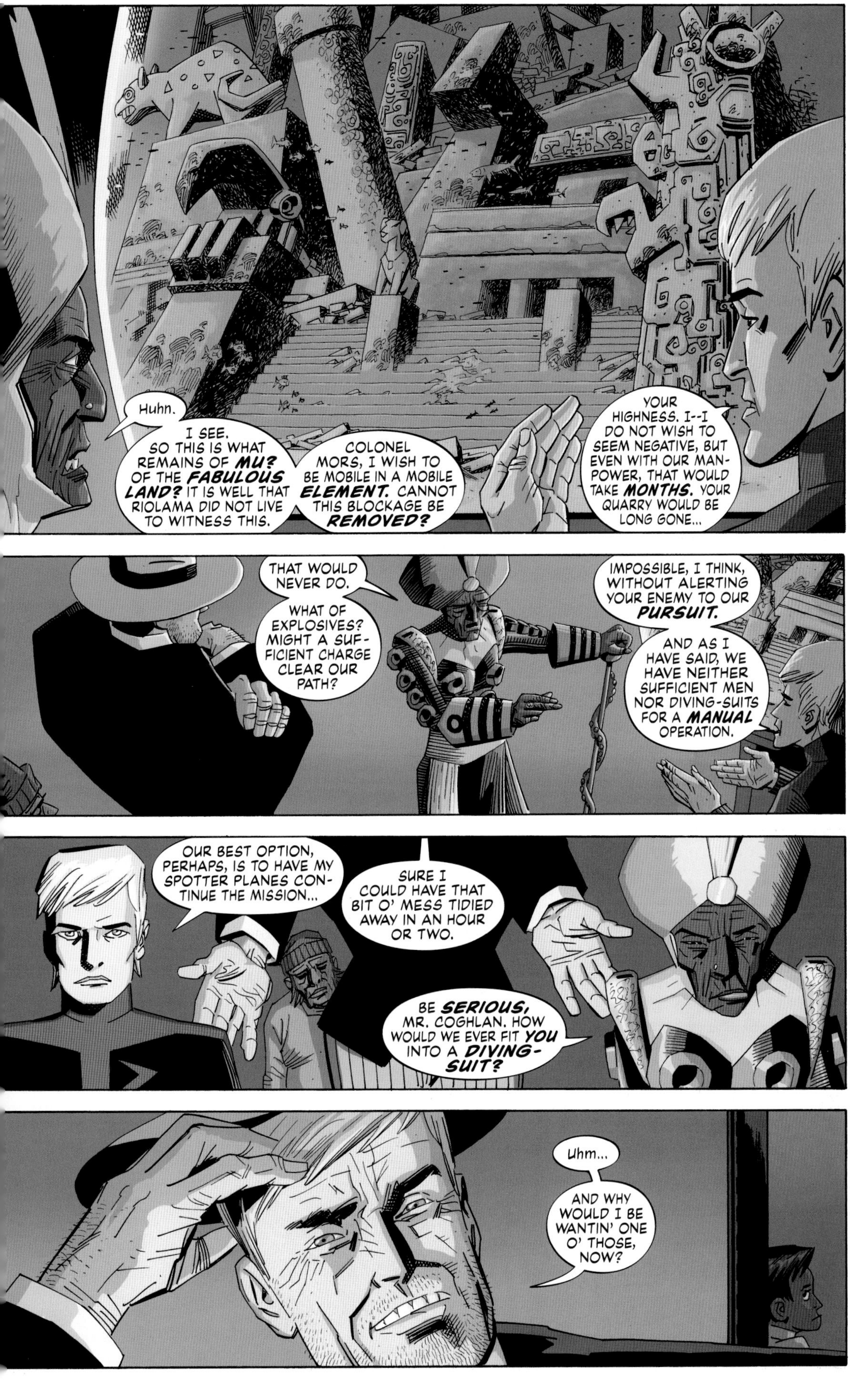
Huhn.
I SEE. SO THIS IS WHAT REMAINS OF MU? OF THE FABULOUS LAND? IT IS WELL THAT RIOLAMA DID NOT LIVE TO WITNESS THIS.
COLONEL MORS, I WISH TO BE MOBILE IN A MOBILE ELEMENT. CANNOT THIS BLOCKAGE BE REMOVED?
YOUR HIGHNESS. I--I DO NOT WISH TO SEEM NEGATIVE, BUT EVEN WITH OUR MAN-POWER, THAT WOULD TAKE MONTHS. YOUR QUARRY WOULD BE LONG GONE...
THAT WOULD NEVER DO.
WHAT OF EXPLOSIVES? MIGHT A SUF-FICIENT CHARGE CLEAR OUR PATH?
IMPOSSIBLE, I THINK, WITHOUT ALERTING YOUR ENEMY TO OUR PURSUIT.
AND AS I HAVE SAID, WE HAVE NEITHER SUFFICIENT MEN NOR DIVING-SUITS FOR A MANUAL OPERATION.
OUR BEST OPTION, PERHAPS, IS TO HAVE MY SPOTTER PLANES CON-TINUE THE MISSION...
SURE I COULD HAVE THAT BIT O' MESS TIDIED AWAY IN AN HOUR OR TWO.
BE SERIOUS, MR. COGHLAN. HOW WOULD WE EVER FIT YOU INTO A DIVING-SUIT?
Uhm...
AND WHY WOULD I BE WANTIN' ONE O' THOSE, NOW?

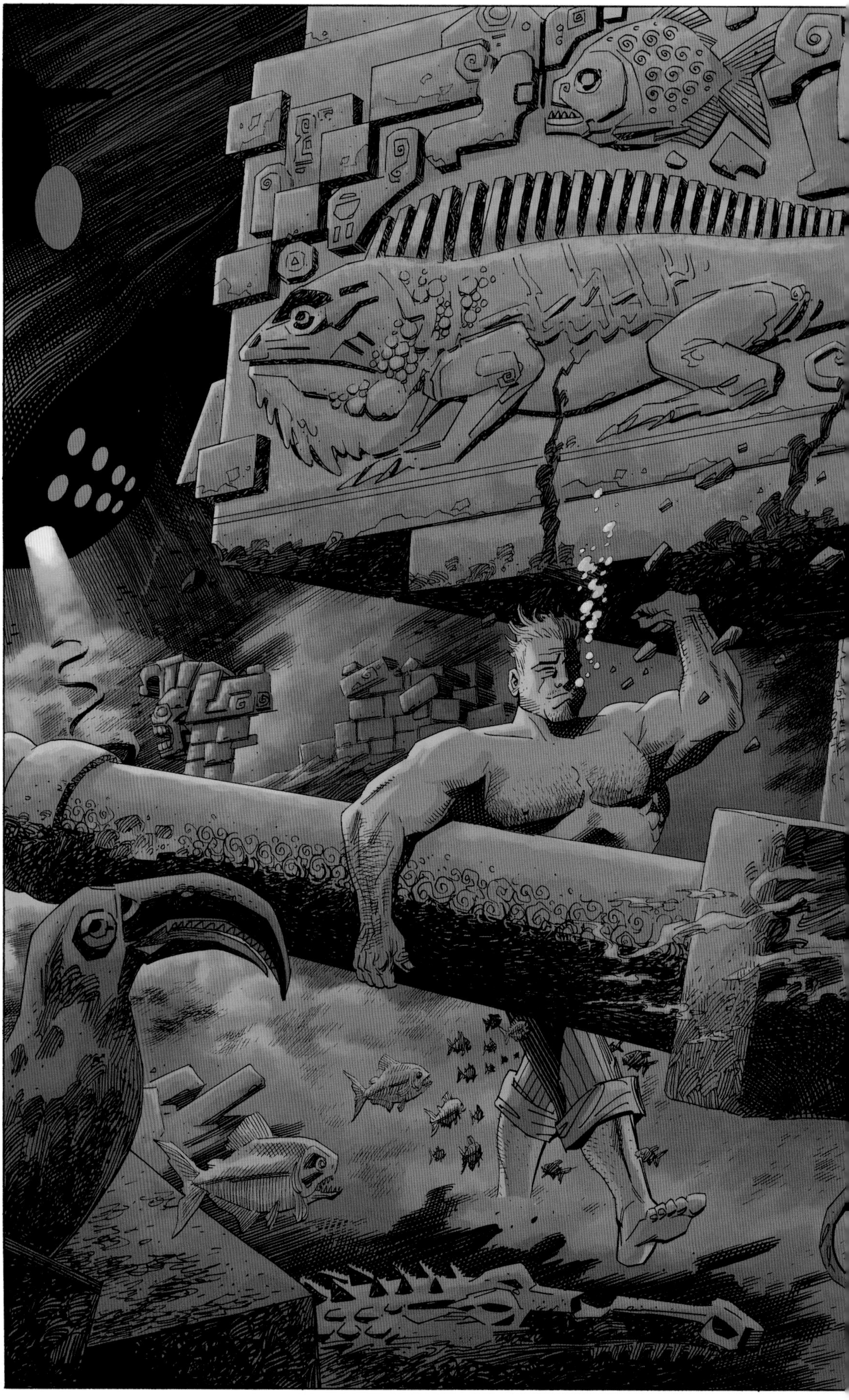

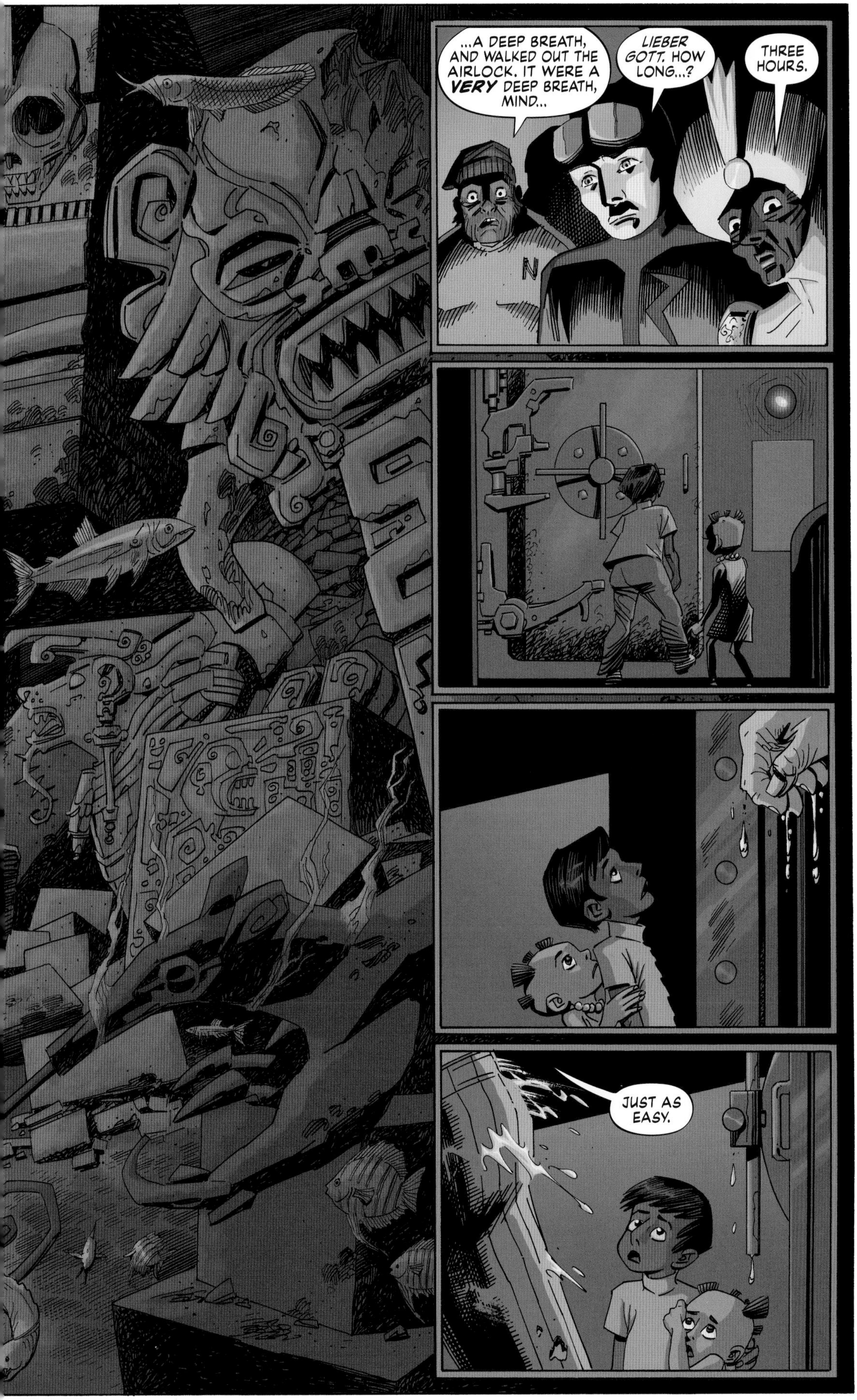
...A DEEP BREATH, AND WALKED OUT THE AIRLOCK. IT WERE A VERY DEEP BREATH, MIND...
LIEBER GOTT. HOW LONG...?
THREE HOURS.
JUST AS EASY.

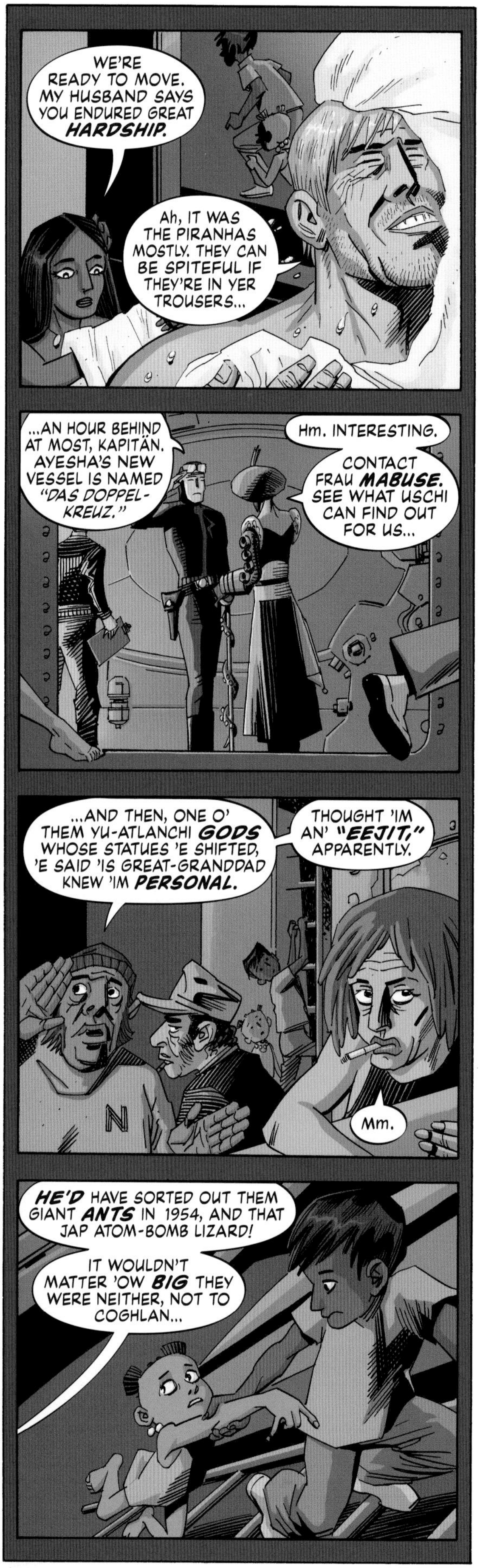

WE'RE READY TO MOVE. MY HUSBAND SAYS YOU ENDURED GREAT HARDSHIP.
Ah, IT WAS THE PIRANHAS MOSTLY. THEY CAN BE SPITEFUL IF THEY'RE IN YER TROUSERS...
...AN HOUR BEHIND AT MOST, KAPITÄN. AYESHA'S NEW VESSEL IS NAMED "DAS DOPPEL-KREUZ."
Hm. INTERESTING.
CONTACT FRAU MABUSE. SEE WHAT USCHI CAN FIND OUT FOR US...
...AND THEN, ONE O' THEM YU-ATLANCHI GODS WHOSE STATUES 'E SHIFTED, 'E SAID 'IS GREAT-GRANDDAD KNEW 'IM PERSONAL.
THOUGHT 'IM AN' "EEJIT," APPARENTLY.
Mm.
HE'D HAVE SORTED OUT THEM GIANT ANTS IN 1954, AND THAT JAP ATOM-BOMB LIZARD!
IT WOULDN'T MATTER 'OW BIG THEY WERE NEITHER, NOT TO COGHLAN...

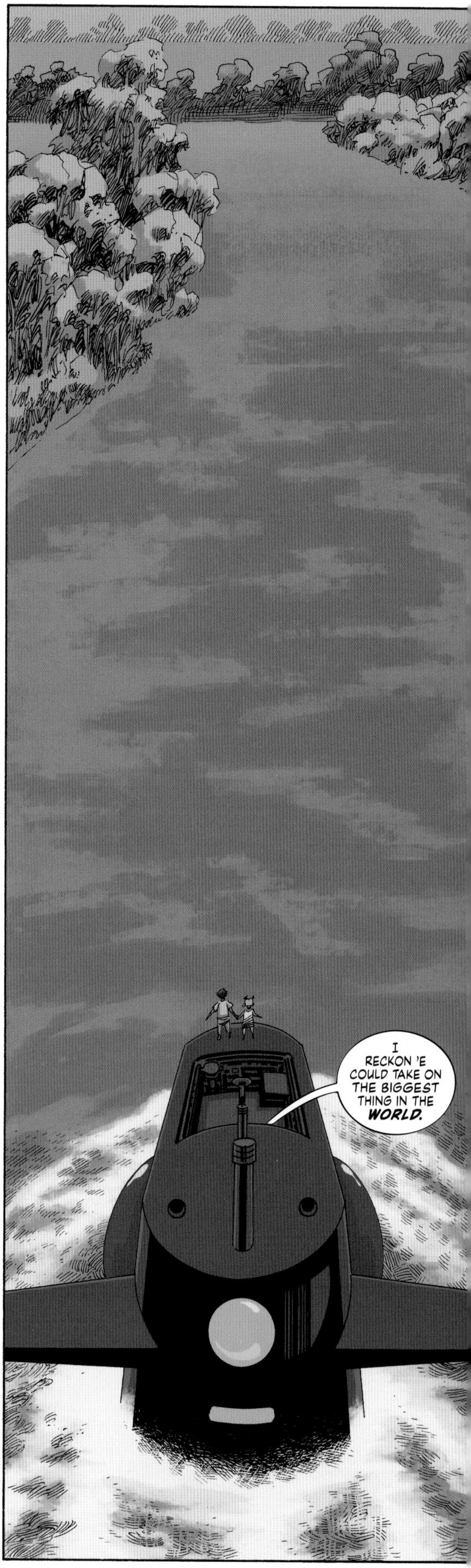

I RECKON 'E COULD TAKE ON THE BIGGEST THING IN THE WORLD.

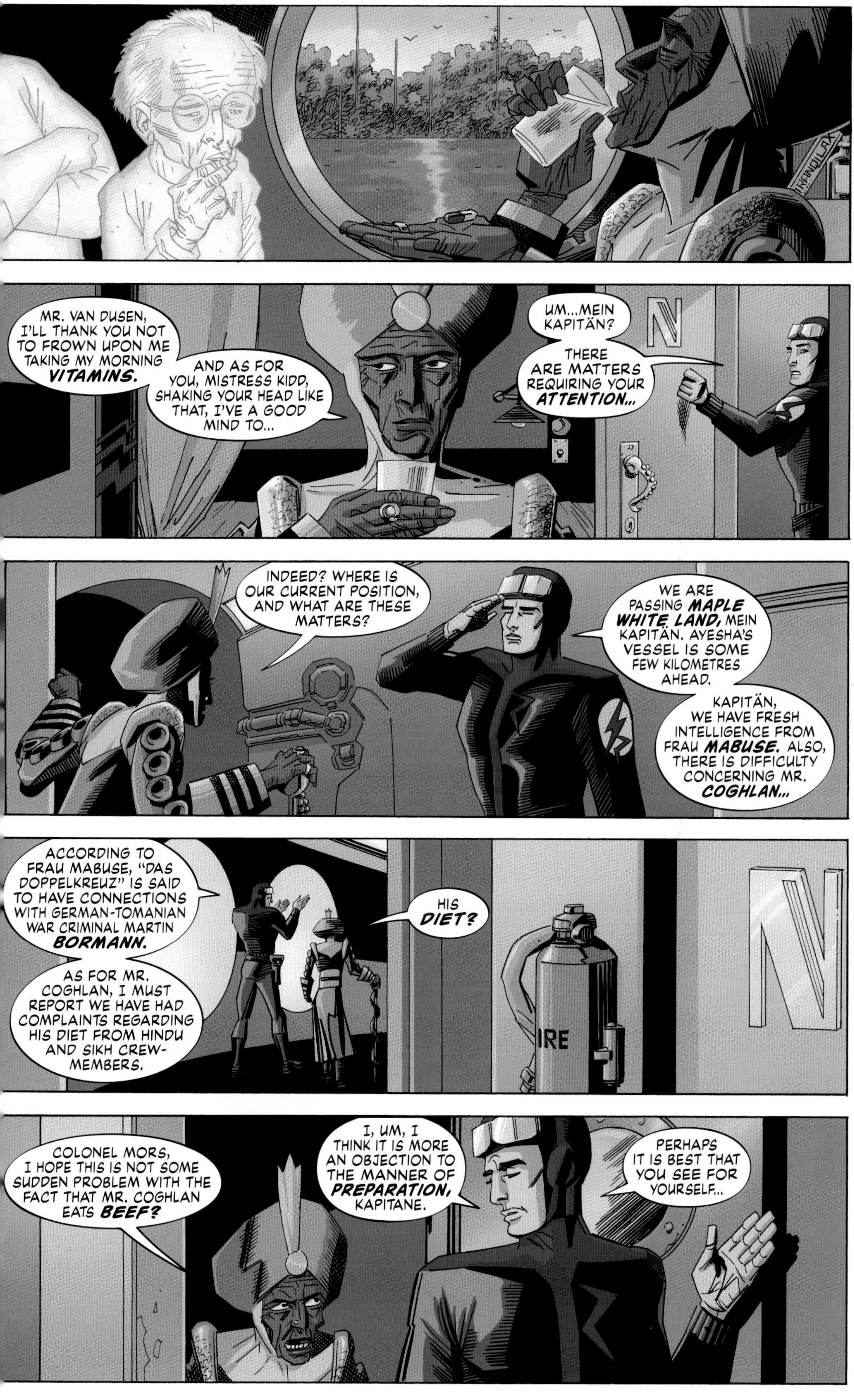
MR. VAN DUSEN, I'LL THANK YOU NOT TO FROWN UPON ME TAKING MY MORNING **VITAMINS.**
AND AS FOR YOU, MISTRESS KIDD, SHAKING YOUR HEAD LIKE THAT, I'VE A GOOD MIND TO...
UM...MEIN KAPITÄN?
THERE ARE MATTERS REQUIRING YOUR **ATTENTION...**
INDEED? WHERE IS OUR CURRENT POSITION, AND WHAT ARE THESE MATTERS?
WE ARE PASSING **MAPLE WHITE LAND,** MEIN KAPITÄN. AYESHA'S VESSEL IS SOME FEW KILOMETRES AHEAD.
KAPITÄN, WE HAVE FRESH INTELLIGENCE FROM FRAU **MABUSE.** ALSO, THERE IS DIFFICULTY CONCERNING MR. **COGHLAN...**
ACCORDING TO FRAU MABUSE, "DAS DOPPELKREUZ" IS SAID TO HAVE CONNECTIONS WITH GERMAN-TOMANIAN WAR CRIMINAL MARTIN **BORMANN.**
AS FOR MR. COGHLAN, I MUST REPORT WE HAVE HAD COMPLAINTS REGARDING HIS DIET FROM HINDU AND SIKH CREW-MEMBERS.
HIS **DIET?**
IRE
COLONEL MORS, I HOPE THIS IS NOT SOME SUDDEN PROBLEM WITH THE FACT THAT MR. COGHLAN EATS **BEEF?**
I, UM, I THINK IT IS MORE AN OBJECTION TO THE MANNER OF **PREPARATION,** KAPITANE.
PERHAPS IT IS BEST THAT YOU SEE FOR YOURSELF...

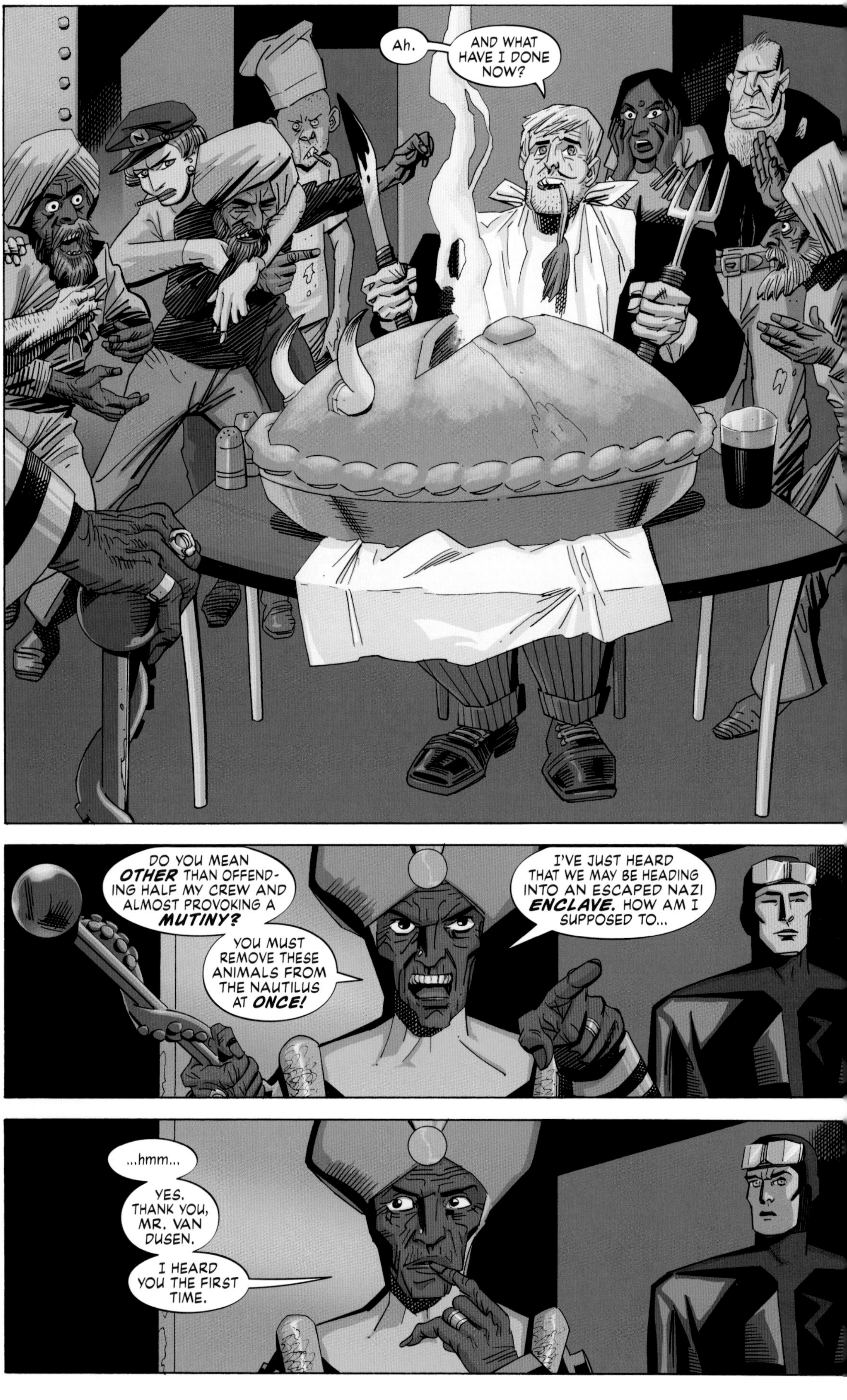
Ah.
AND WHAT HAVE I DONE NOW?
DO YOU MEAN OTHER THAN OFFENDING HALF MY CREW AND ALMOST PROVOKING A MUTINY?
YOU MUST REMOVE THESE ANIMALS FROM THE NAUTILUS AT ONCE!
I'VE JUST HEARD THAT WE MAY BE HEADING INTO AN ESCAPED NAZI ENCLAVE. HOW AM I SUPPOSED TO...
...hmm...
YES. THANK YOU, MR. VAN DUSEN.
I HEARD YOU THE FIRST TIME.

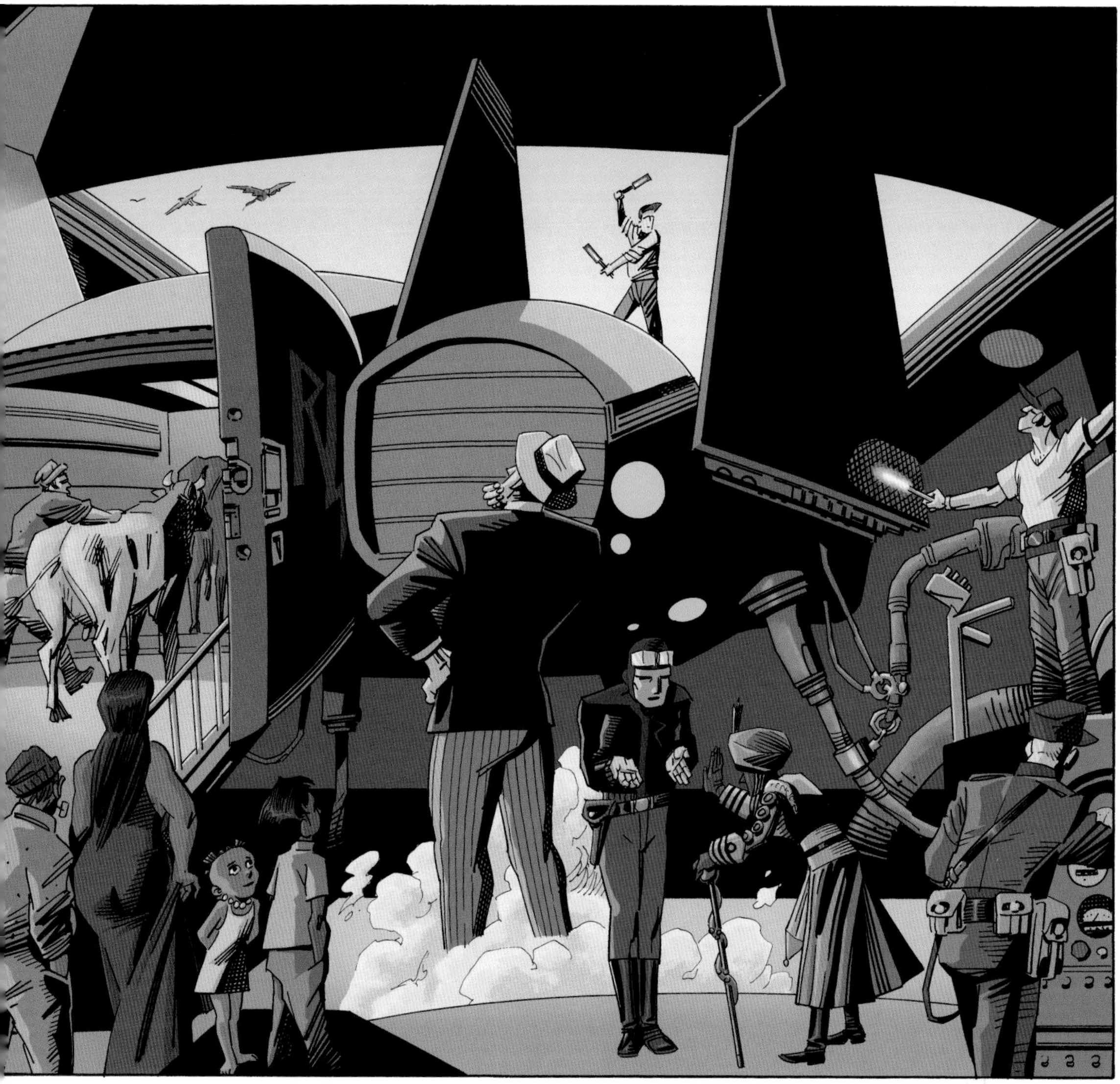

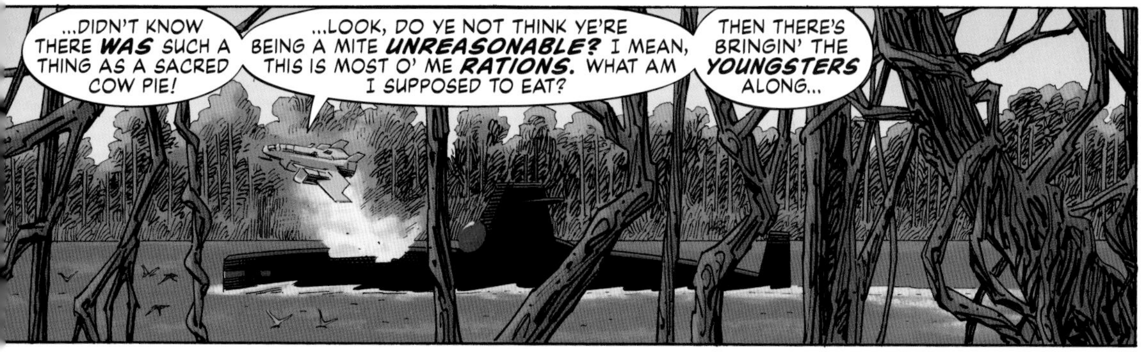
...DIDN'T KNOW THERE WAS SUCH A THING AS A SACRED COW PIE!
...LOOK, DO YE NOT THINK YE'RE BEING A MITE UNREASONABLE? I MEAN, THIS IS MOST O' ME RATIONS. WHAT AM I SUPPOSED TO EAT?
THEN THERE'S BRINGIN' THE YOUNGSTERS ALONG...

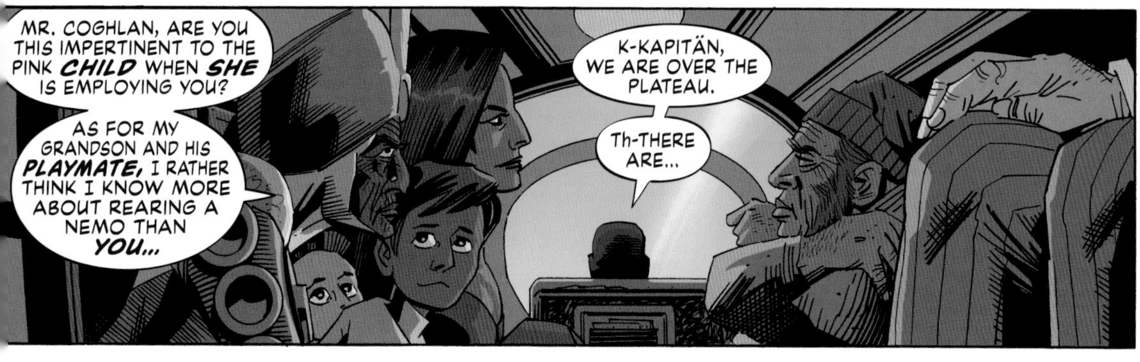
MR. COGHLAN, ARE YOU THIS IMPERTINENT TO THE PINK CHILD WHEN SHE IS EMPLOYING YOU?
AS FOR MY GRANDSON AND HIS PLAYMATE, I RATHER THINK I KNOW MORE ABOUT REARING A NEMO THAN YOU...
K-KAPITÄN, WE ARE OVER THE PLATEAU.
Th-THERE ARE...

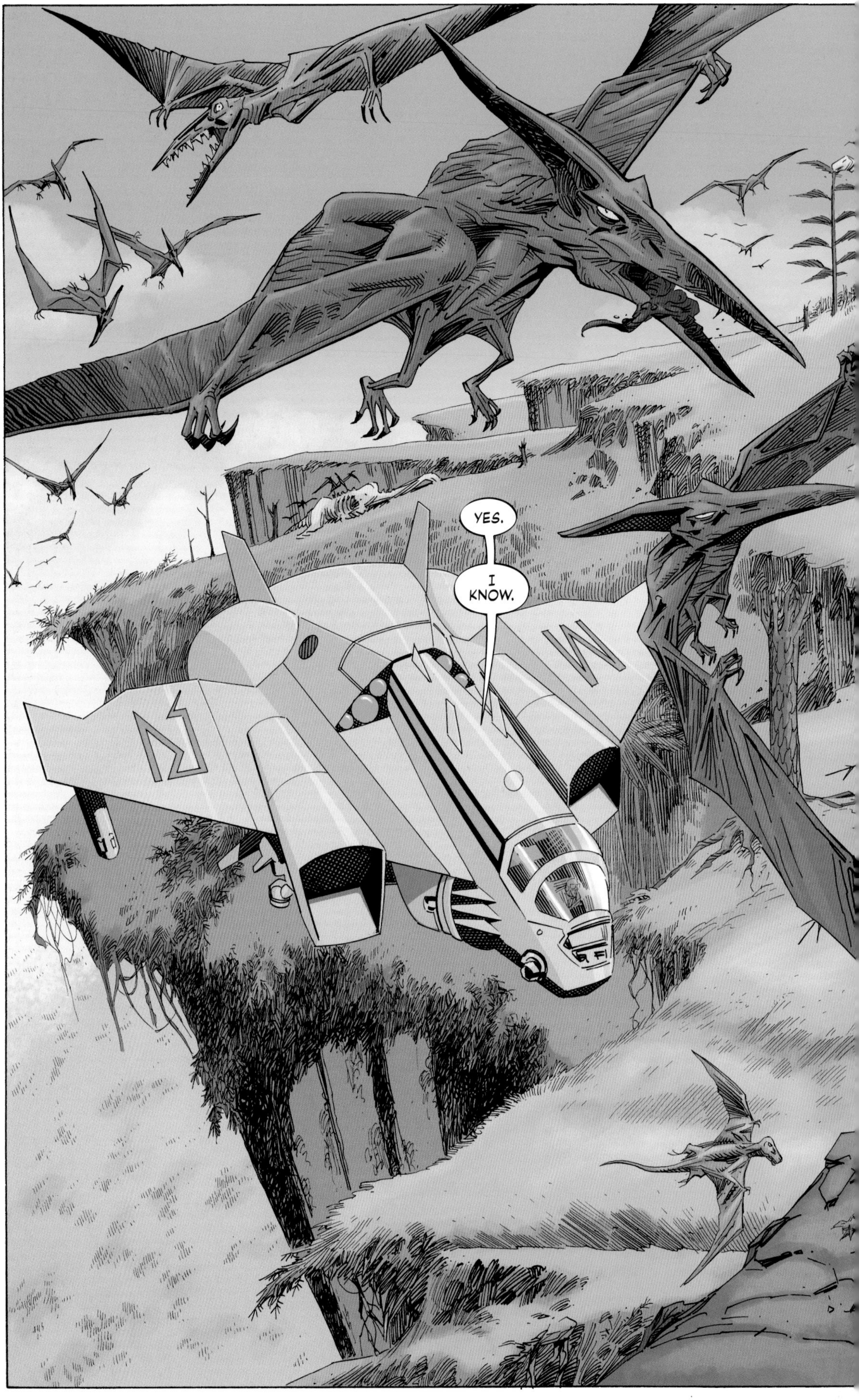
YES.
I KNOW.

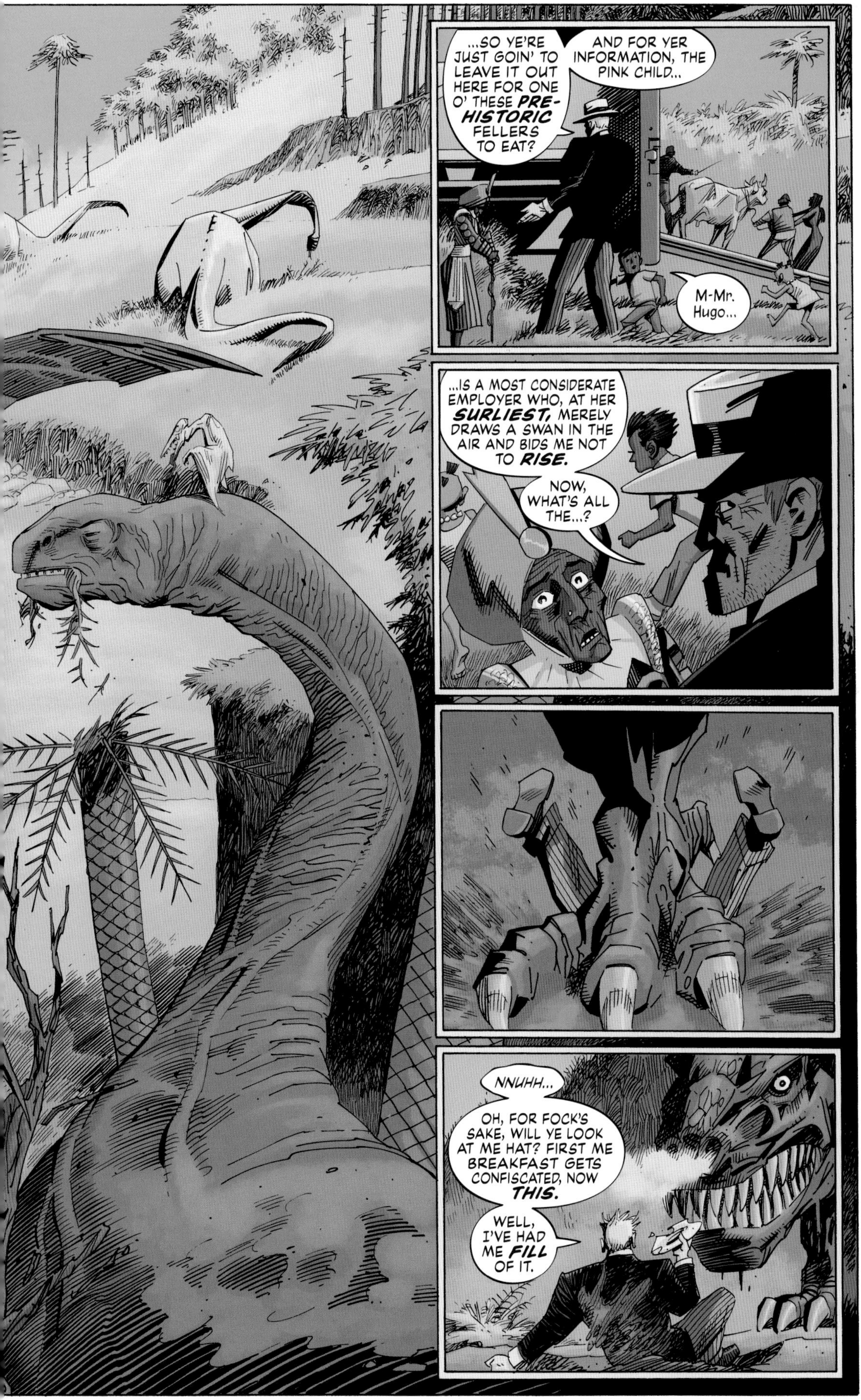
...SO YE'RE JUST GOIN' TO LEAVE IT OUT HERE FOR ONE O' THESE PRE-HISTORIC FELLERS TO EAT?
AND FOR YER INFORMATION, THE PINK CHILD...
M-Mr. Hugo...
...IS A MOST CONSIDERATE EMPLOYER WHO, AT HER SURLIEST, MERELY DRAWS A SWAN IN THE AIR AND BIDS ME NOT TO RISE.
NOW, WHAT'S ALL THE...?
NNUHH...
OH, FOR FOCK'S SAKE, WILL YE LOOK AT ME HAT? FIRST ME BREAKFAST GETS CONFISCATED, NOW THIS.
WELL, I'VE HAD ME FILL OF IT.

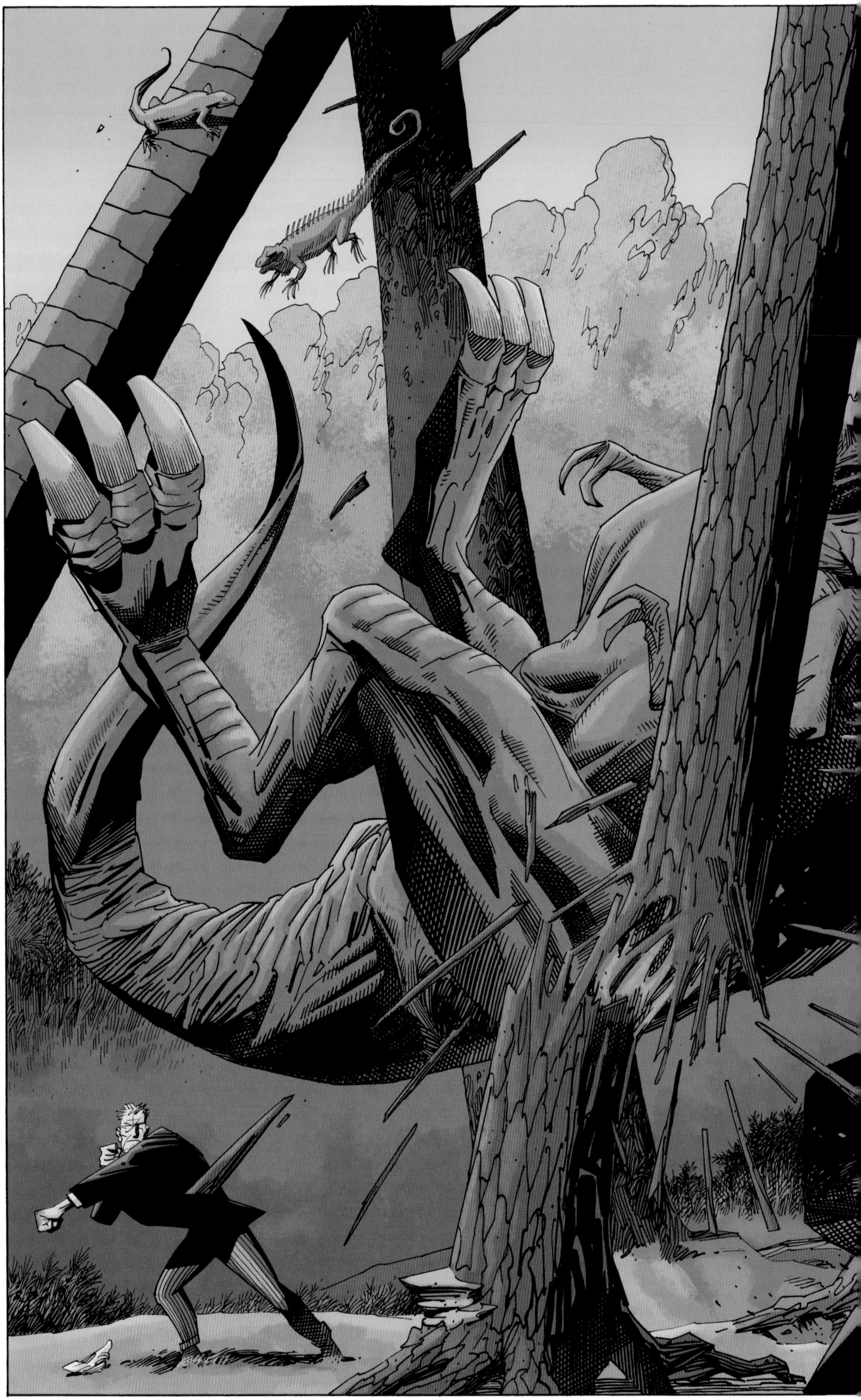

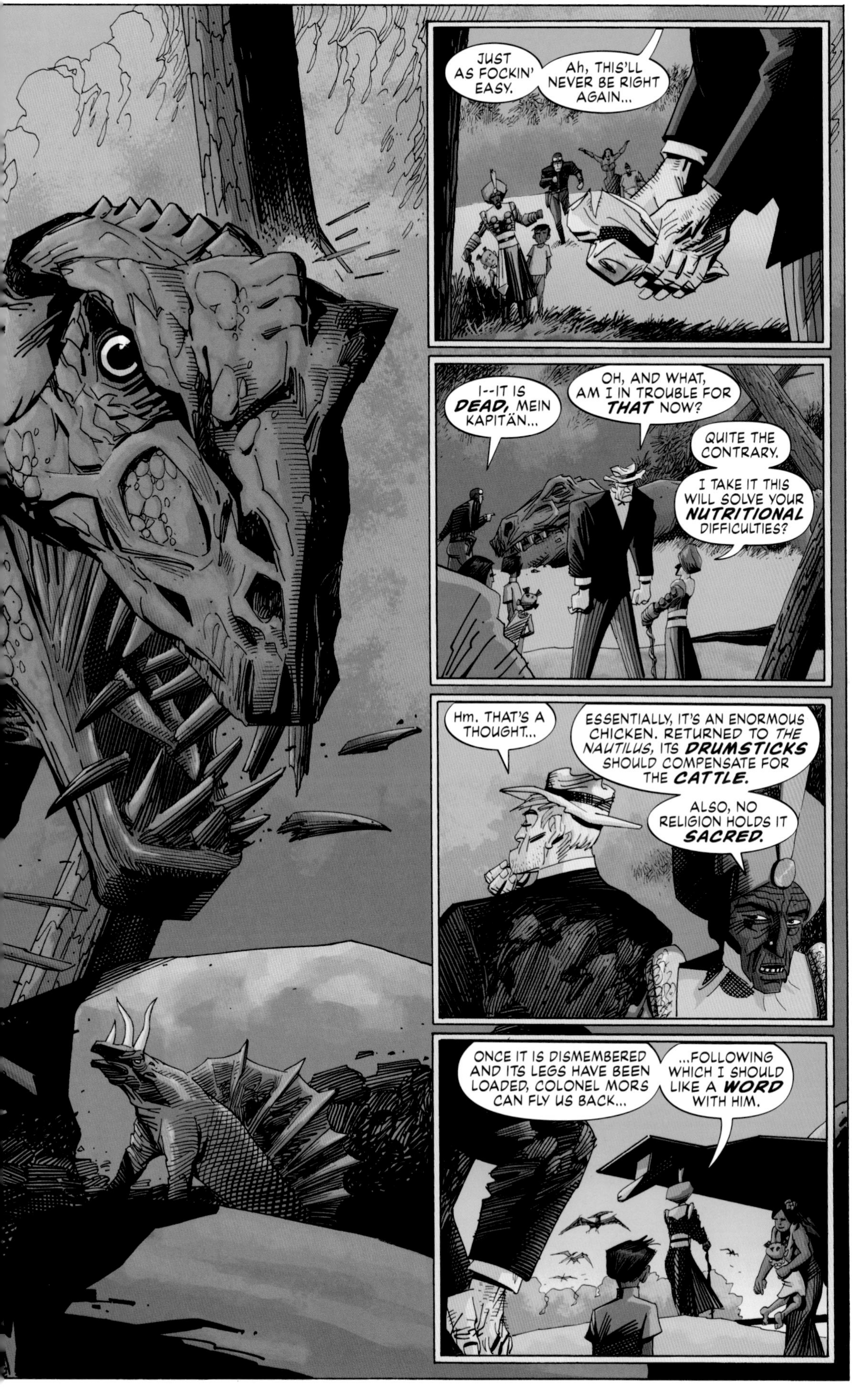

JUST AS FOCKIN' EASY.
Ah, THIS'LL NEVER BE RIGHT AGAIN...
I--IT IS **DEAD,** MEIN KAPITÄN...
OH, AND WHAT, AM I IN TROUBLE FOR **THAT** NOW?
QUITE THE CONTRARY.
I TAKE IT THIS WILL SOLVE YOUR **NUTRITIONAL** DIFFICULTIES?
Hm. THAT'S A THOUGHT...
ESSENTIALLY, IT'S AN ENORMOUS CHICKEN. RETURNED TO *THE NAUTILUS,* ITS **DRUMSTICKS** SHOULD COMPENSATE FOR THE **CATTLE.**
ALSO, NO RELIGION HOLDS IT **SACRED.**
ONCE IT IS DISMEMBERED AND ITS LEGS HAVE BEEN LOADED, COLONEL MORS CAN FLY US BACK...
...FOLLOWING WHICH I SHOULD LIKE A **WORD** WITH HIM.

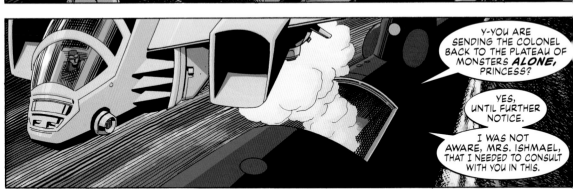

Y-YOU ARE SENDING THE COLONEL BACK TO THE PLATEAU OF MONSTERS *ALONE*, PRINCESS?

YES, UNTIL FURTHER NOTICE.

I WAS NOT AWARE, MRS. ISHMAEL, THAT I NEEDED TO CONSULT WITH YOU IN THIS.

N-NO, CAPTAIN. LUALA WEREN'T MEANIN' THAT. I-IT'S JUST, THE COLONEL'S ABOUT OUR BEST MAN, AND IF THIS IS REGARDIN' MISTRESS *HIRA*...

DO NOT *PROVOKE* ME, MR. ISHMAEL. AND JACK, I'LL THANK *YOU* NOT TO *INTERRUPT* MY CONVERSATIONS...

B-But... I didn't say anything.

I WASN'T TALKING TO YOU.

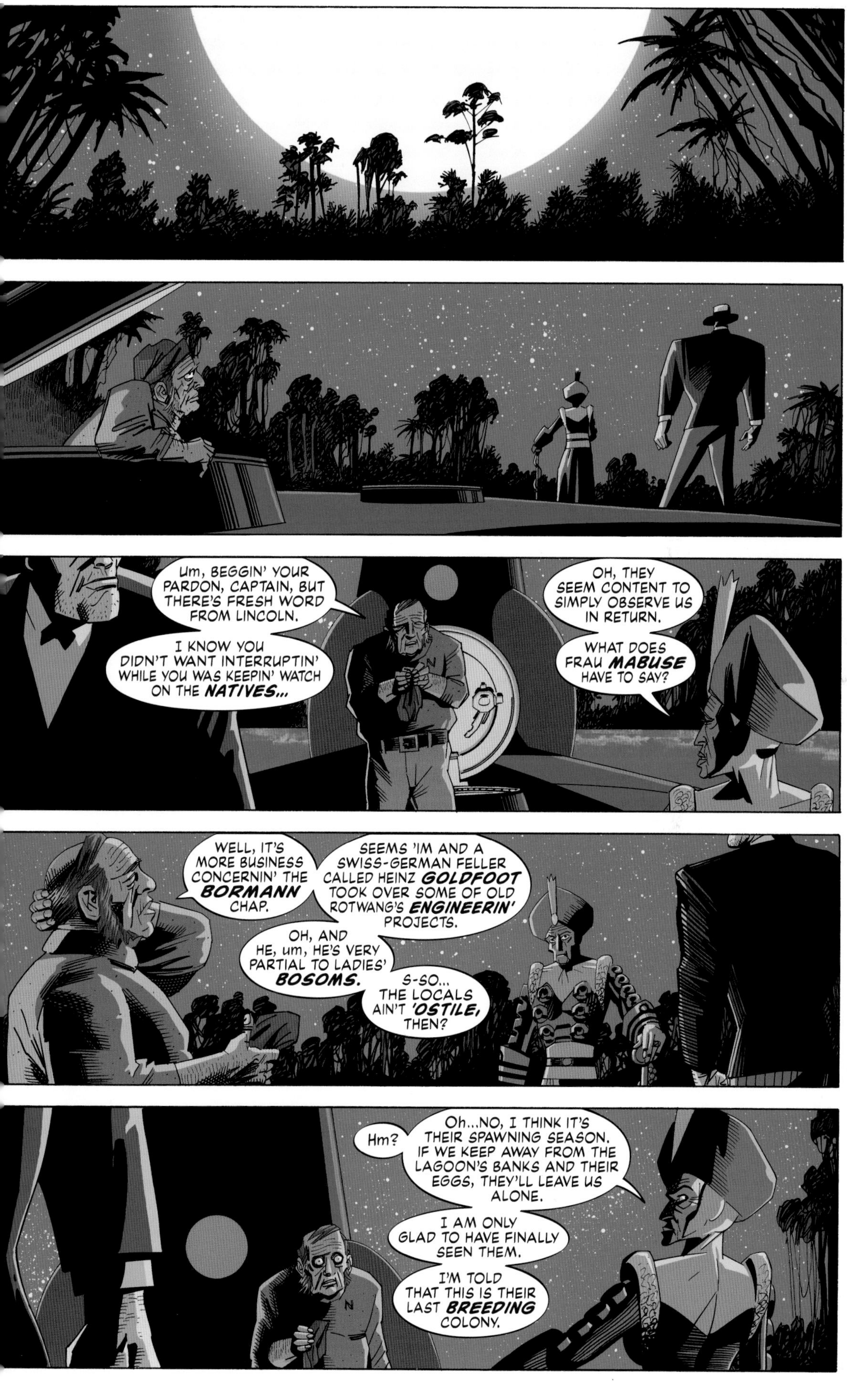

Um, BEGGIN' YOUR PARDON, CAPTAIN, BUT THERE'S FRESH WORD FROM LINCOLN.
I KNOW YOU DIDN'T WANT INTERRUPTIN' WHILE YOU WAS KEEPIN' WATCH ON THE NATIVES...
OH, THEY SEEM CONTENT TO SIMPLY OBSERVE US IN RETURN.
WHAT DOES FRAU MABUSE HAVE TO SAY?
WELL, IT'S MORE BUSINESS CONCERNIN' THE BORMANN CHAP.
SEEMS 'IM AND A SWISS-GERMAN FELLER CALLED HEINZ GOLDFOOT TOOK OVER SOME OF OLD ROTWANG'S ENGINEERIN' PROJECTS.
OH, AND HE, um, HE'S VERY PARTIAL TO LADIES' BOSOMS.
S-SO... THE LOCALS AIN'T 'OSTILE, THEN?
Hm?
Oh...NO, I THINK IT'S THEIR SPAWNING SEASON. IF WE KEEP AWAY FROM THE LAGOON'S BANKS AND THEIR EGGS, THEY'LL LEAVE US ALONE.
I AM ONLY GLAD TO HAVE FINALLY SEEN THEM.
I'M TOLD THAT THIS IS THEIR LAST BREEDING COLONY.

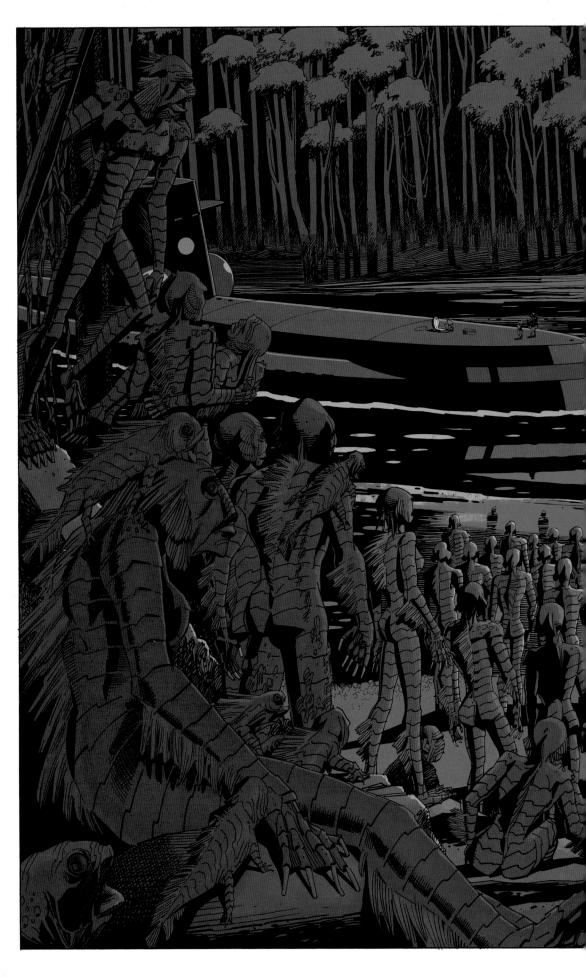

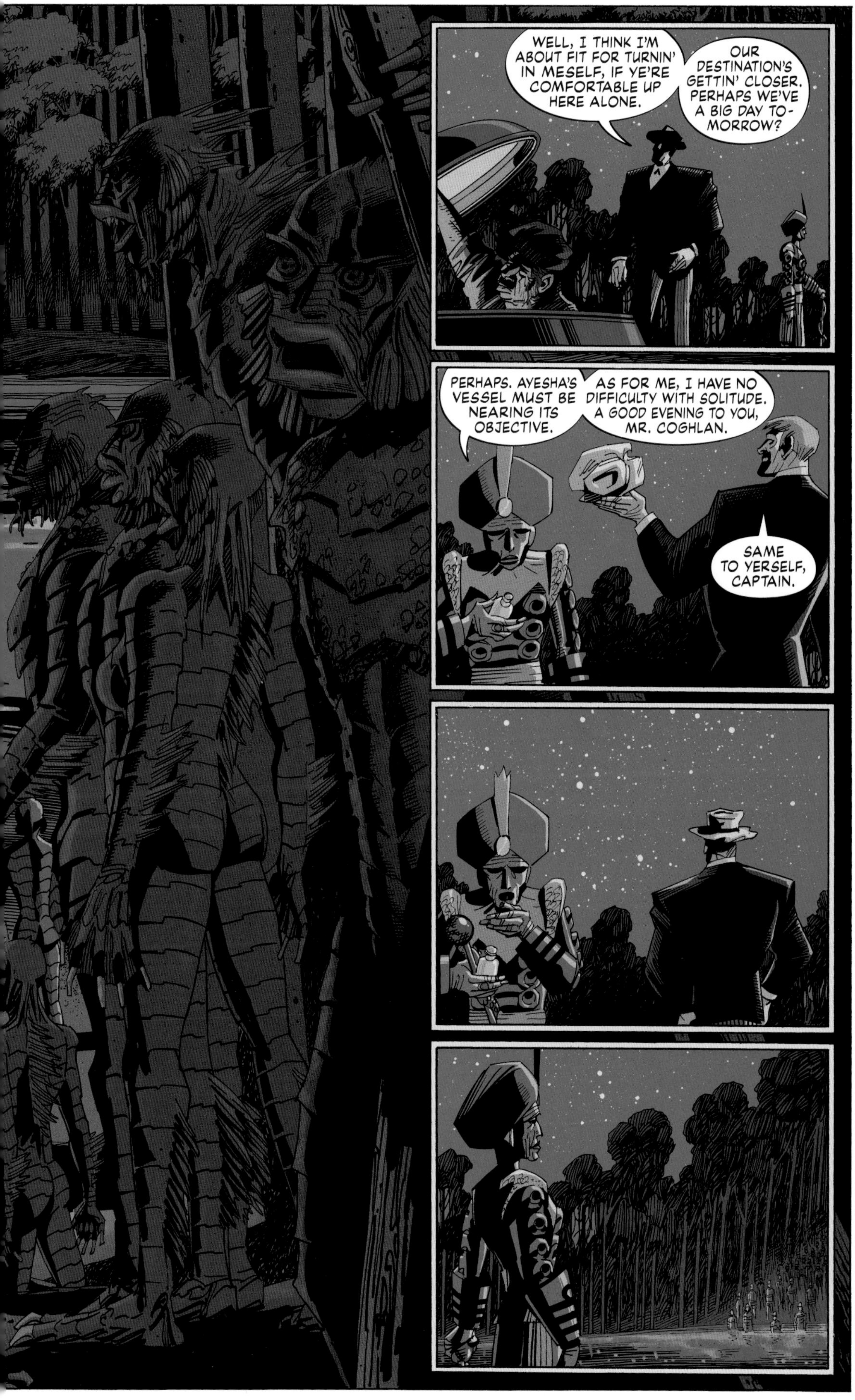
WELL, I THINK I'M ABOUT FIT FOR TURNIN' IN MESELF, IF YE'RE COMFORTABLE UP HERE ALONE.
OUR DESTINATION'S GETTIN' CLOSER. PERHAPS WE'VE A BIG DAY TO-MORROW?
PERHAPS. AYESHA'S VESSEL MUST BE NEARING ITS OBJECTIVE.
AS FOR ME, I HAVE NO DIFFICULTY WITH SOLITUDE. A GOOD EVENING TO YOU, MR. COGHLAN.
SAME TO YERSELF, CAPTAIN.

CAPTAIN? LOOKS LIKE SHE'S PUTTIN' IN TO SHORE, ACCORDIN' TO THE *SONAR*.

THEN CUT THE ENGINES. IF SHE IS WITHIN REACH OF *OUR* INSTRUMENTS, WE MAY BE IN REACH OF HER *HOSTS'*.

WE'LL FOLLOW FROM HERE IN THE *NAUTILOIDS*. PREPARE THEM BOTH.

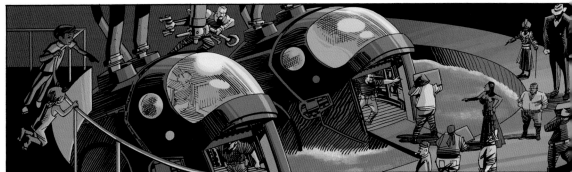

Ah! THERE SHE IS. JUST AS I REMEMBER HER, AND YET...

...THERE'S SOMETHING DIFFERENT ABOUT HER EYES. IS IT THAT THEY LOOK *OLDER?*

SURE I WOULDN'T KNOW. I'VE NEVER MET THE WOMAN.

NOT MUCH *LEG ROOM* IN THESE THINGS, IS THERE, NOW?

PRINCESS, SHE IS BOARDING A TOMANIAN ARMOURED CAR. THE NAUTILUS WILL LOSE VISUAL CONTACT...

WE CAN TRACK THEM BY THEIR VEHICLE'S ELECTRICS. HOPEFULLY, IT'S ONLY MARGINALLY FASTER THAN OUR OWN.

THANK YOU, MRS. ISHMAEL. THEN WE HAD BEST PUT TO SHORE *OUR-SELVES.*

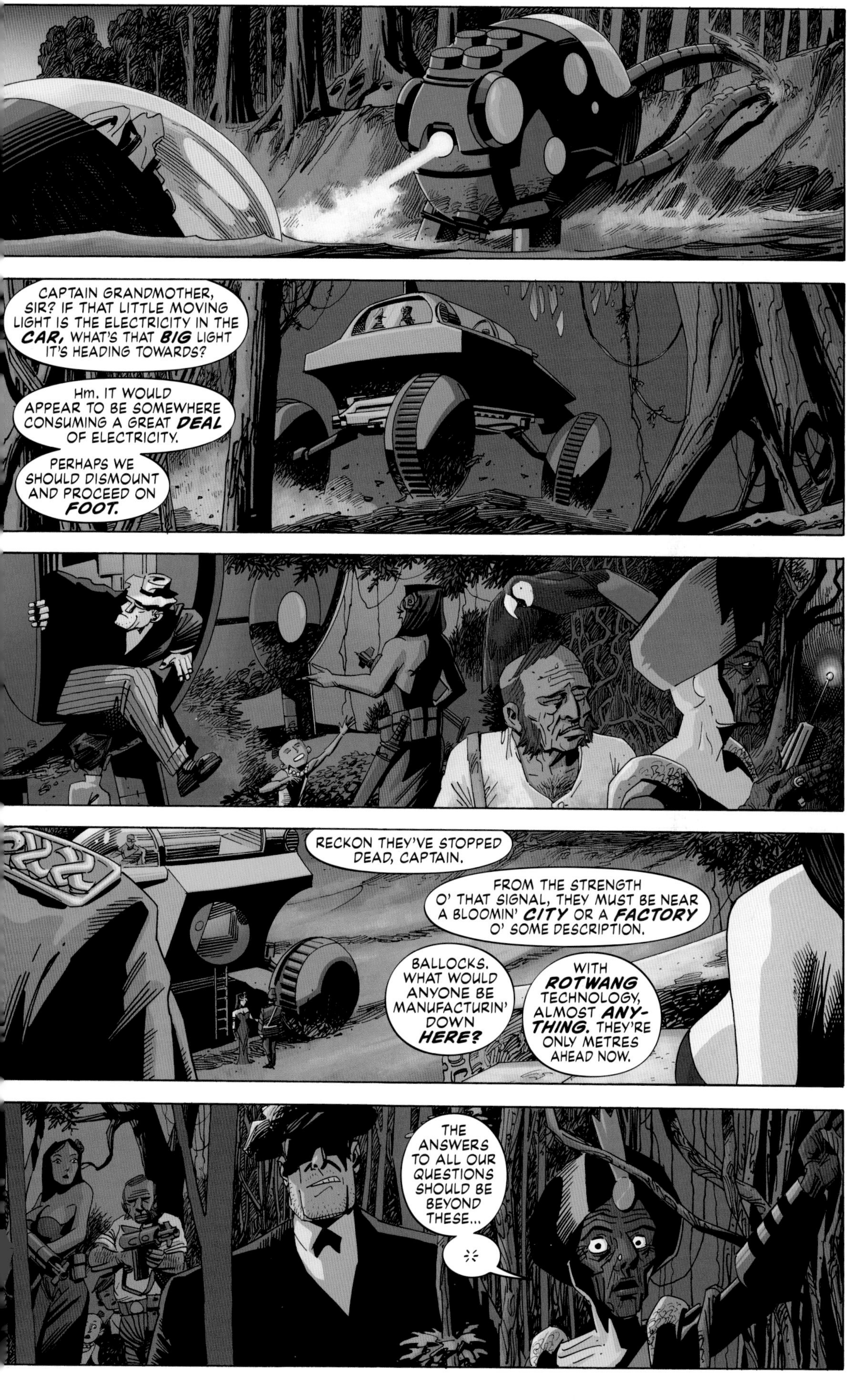
CAPTAIN GRANDMOTHER, SIR? IF THAT LITTLE MOVING LIGHT IS THE ELECTRICITY IN THE CAR, WHAT'S THAT BIG LIGHT IT'S HEADING TOWARDS?
Hm. IT WOULD APPEAR TO BE SOMEWHERE CONSUMING A GREAT DEAL OF ELECTRICITY.
PERHAPS WE SHOULD DISMOUNT AND PROCEED ON FOOT.
RECKON THEY'VE STOPPED DEAD, CAPTAIN.
FROM THE STRENGTH O' THAT SIGNAL, THEY MUST BE NEAR A BLOOMIN' CITY OR A FACTORY O' SOME DESCRIPTION.
BALLOCKS. WHAT WOULD ANYONE BE MANUFACTURIN' DOWN HERE?
WITH ROTWANG TECHNOLOGY, ALMOST ANY-THING. THEY'RE ONLY METRES AHEAD NOW.
THE ANSWERS TO ALL OUR QUESTIONS SHOULD BE BEYOND THESE...

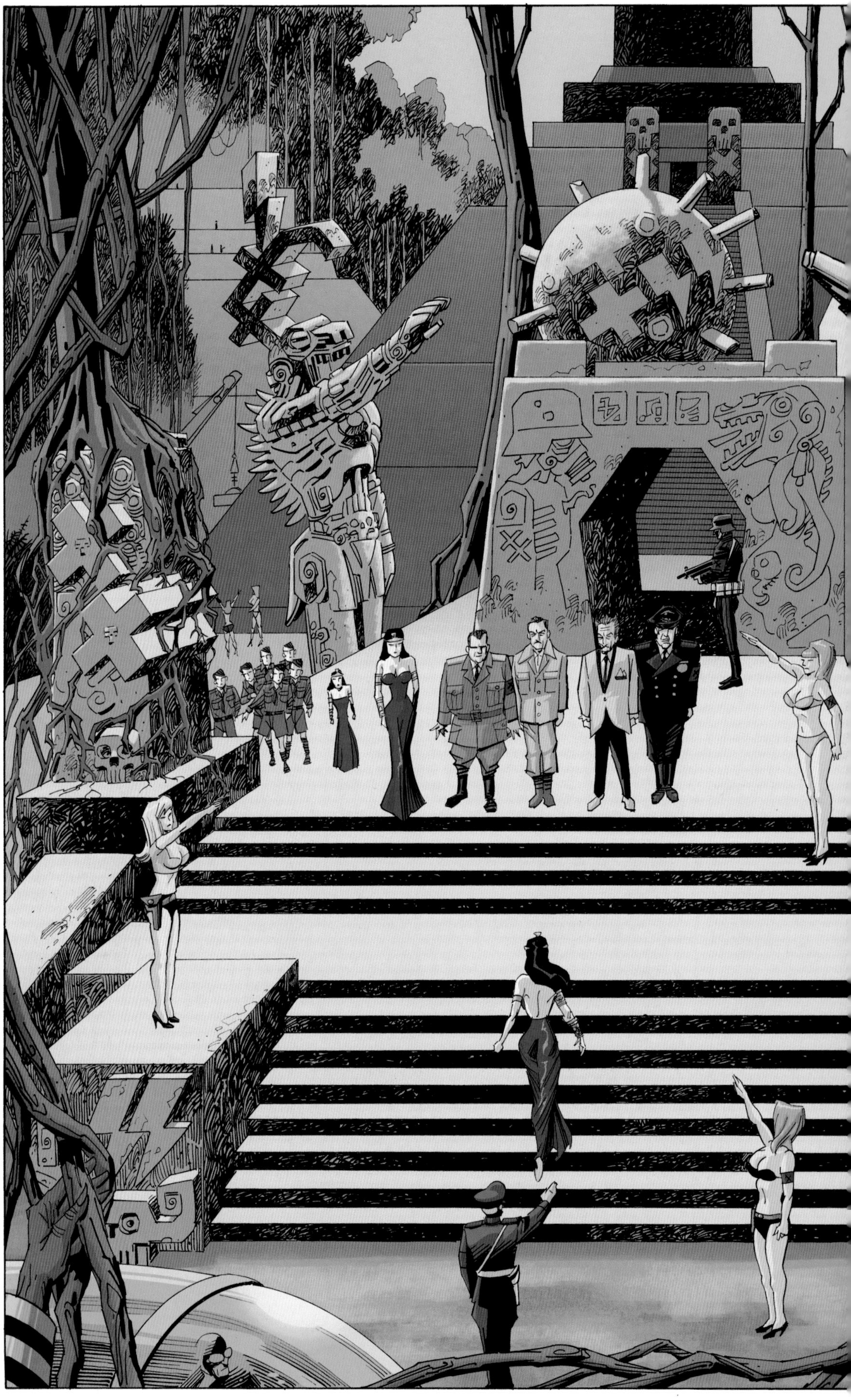

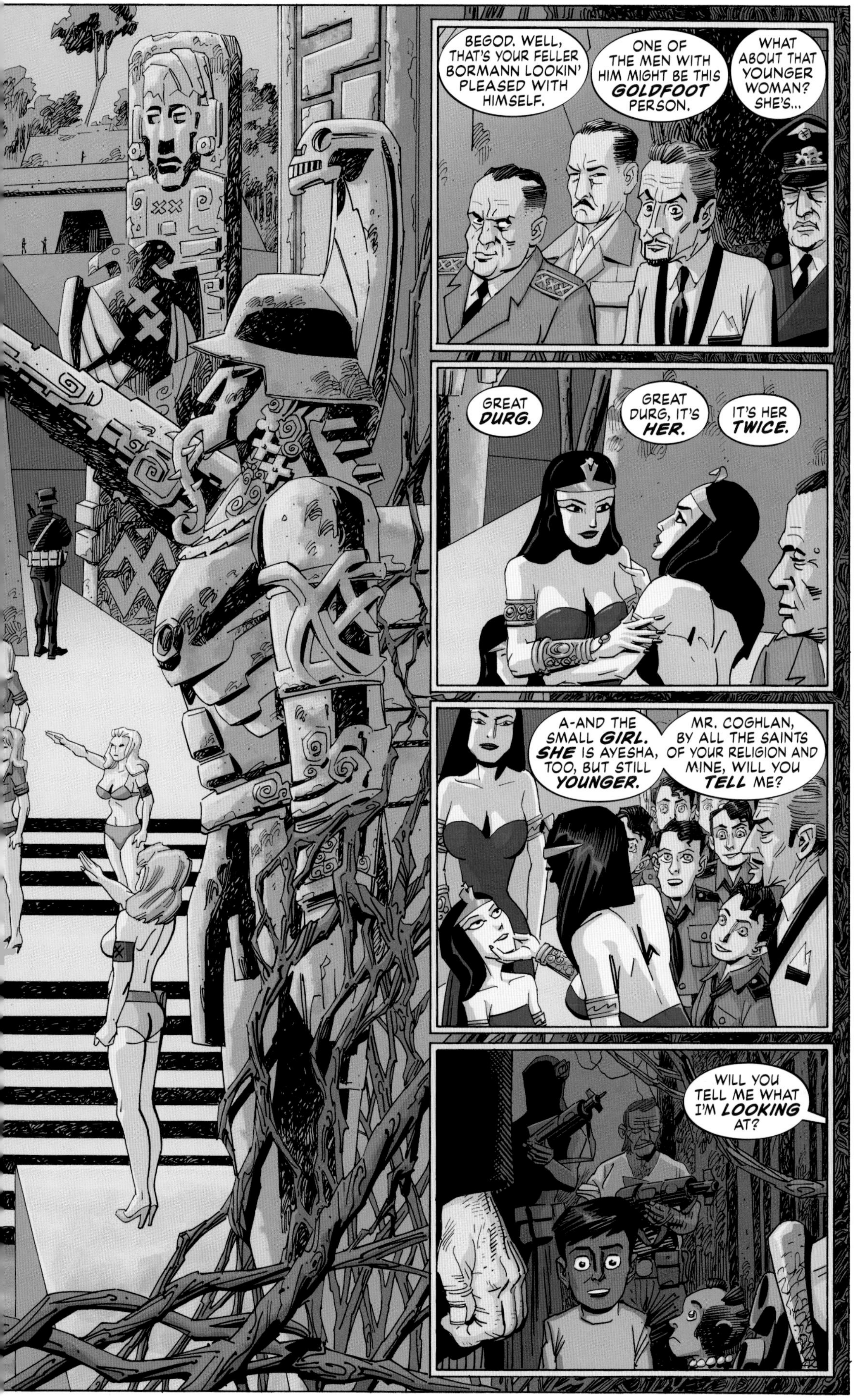
BEGOD. WELL, THAT'S YOUR FELLER BORMANN LOOKIN' PLEASED WITH HIMSELF.
ONE OF THE MEN WITH HIM MIGHT BE THIS GOLDFOOT PERSON.
WHAT ABOUT THAT YOUNGER WOMAN? SHE'S...
GREAT DURG.
GREAT DURG, IT'S HER.
IT'S HER TWICE.
A-AND THE SMALL GIRL. SHE IS AYESHA, TOO, BUT STILL YOUNGER.
MR. COGHLAN, BY ALL THE SAINTS OF YOUR RELIGION AND MINE, WILL YOU TELL ME?
WILL YOU TELL ME WHAT I'M LOOKING AT?

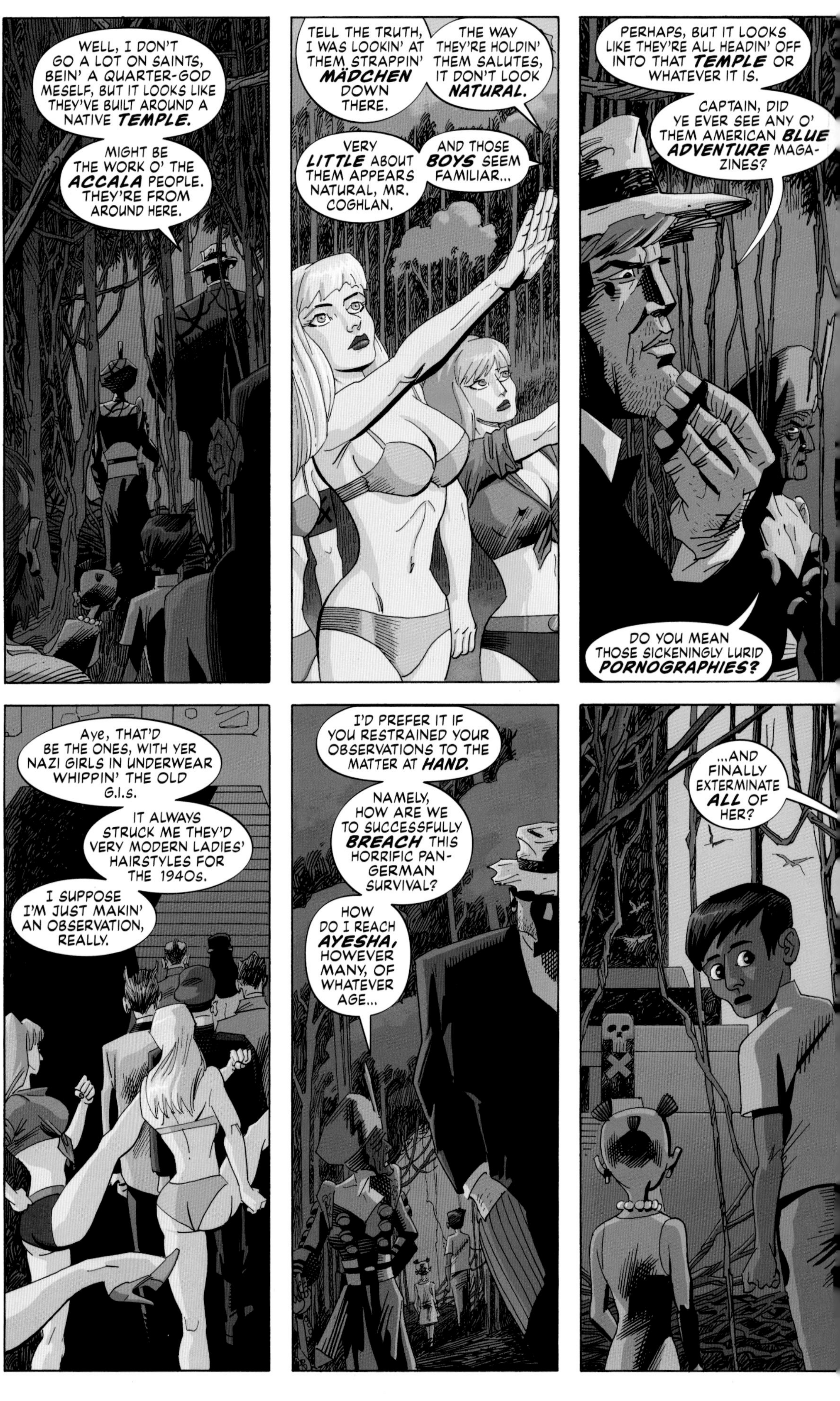
WELL, I DON'T GO A LOT ON SAINTS, BEIN' A QUARTER-GOD MESELF, BUT IT LOOKS LIKE THEY'VE BUILT AROUND A NATIVE TEMPLE.
MIGHT BE THE WORK O' THE ACCALA PEOPLE. THEY'RE FROM AROUND HERE.
TELL THE TRUTH, I WAS LOOKIN' AT THEM STRAPPIN' MÄDCHEN DOWN THERE.
THE WAY THEY'RE HOLDIN' THEM SALUTES, IT DON'T LOOK NATURAL.
VERY LITTLE ABOUT THEM APPEARS NATURAL, MR. COGHLAN.
AND THOSE BOYS SEEM FAMILIAR...
PERHAPS, BUT IT LOOKS LIKE THEY'RE ALL HEADIN' OFF INTO THAT TEMPLE OR WHATEVER IT IS.
CAPTAIN, DID YE EVER SEE ANY O' THEM AMERICAN BLUE ADVENTURE MAGA-ZINES?
DO YOU MEAN THOSE SICKENINGLY LURID PORNOGRAPHIES?
Aye, THAT'D BE THE ONES, WITH YER NAZI GIRLS IN UNDERWEAR WHIPPIN' THE OLD G.I.s.
IT ALWAYS STRUCK ME THEY'D VERY MODERN LADIES' HAIRSTYLES FOR THE 1940s.
I SUPPOSE I'M JUST MAKIN' AN OBSERVATION, REALLY.
I'D PREFER IT IF YOU RESTRAINED YOUR OBSERVATIONS TO THE MATTER AT HAND.
NAMELY, HOW ARE WE TO SUCCESSFULLY BREACH THIS HORRIFIC PAN-GERMAN SURVIVAL?
HOW DO I REACH AYESHA, HOWEVER MANY, OF WHATEVER AGE...
...AND FINALLY EXTERMINATE ALL OF HER?

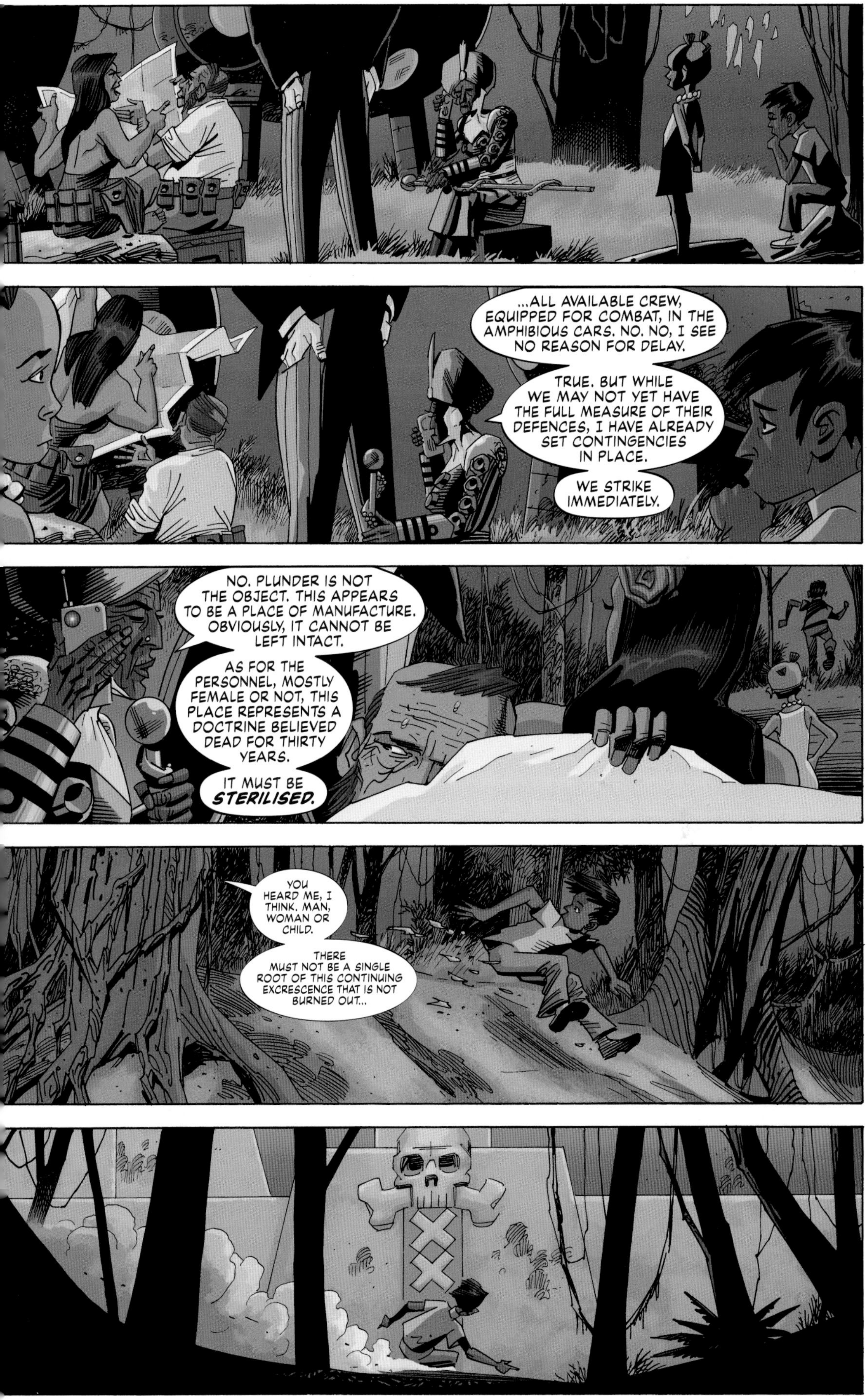
...ALL AVAILABLE CREW, EQUIPPED FOR COMBAT, IN THE AMPHIBIOUS CARS. NO. NO, I SEE NO REASON FOR DELAY.
TRUE. BUT WHILE WE MAY NOT YET HAVE THE FULL MEASURE OF THEIR DEFENCES, I HAVE ALREADY SET CONTINGENCIES IN PLACE.
WE STRIKE IMMEDIATELY.
NO. PLUNDER IS NOT THE OBJECT. THIS APPEARS TO BE A PLACE OF MANUFACTURE. OBVIOUSLY, IT CANNOT BE LEFT INTACT.
AS FOR THE PERSONNEL, MOSTLY FEMALE OR NOT, THIS PLACE REPRESENTS A DOCTRINE BELIEVED DEAD FOR THIRTY YEARS.
IT MUST BE ***STERILISED.***
YOU HEARD ME, I THINK. MAN, WOMAN OR CHILD.
THERE MUST NOT BE A SINGLE ROOT OF THIS CONTINUING EXCRESCENCE THAT IS NOT BURNED OUT...

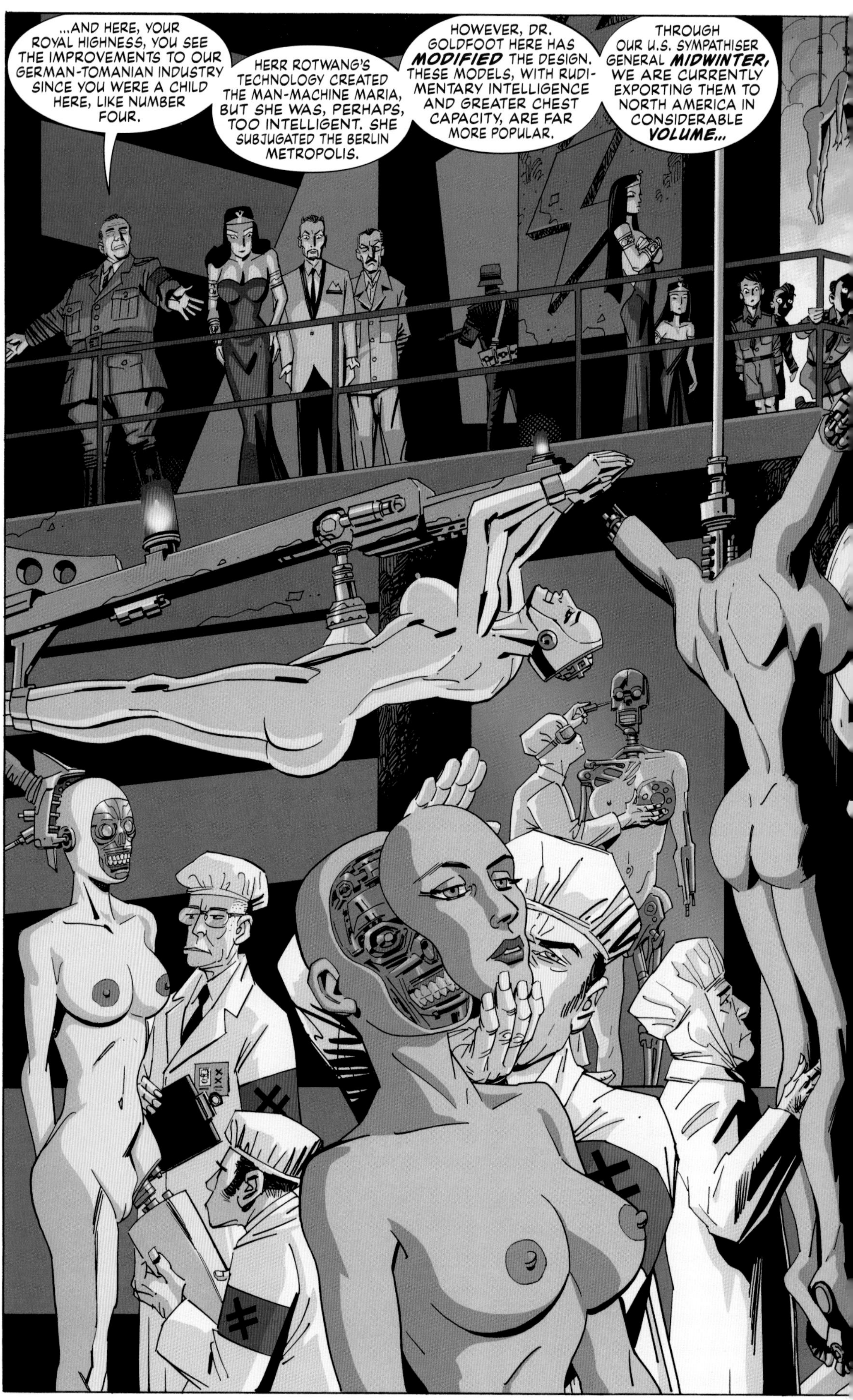
...AND HERE, YOUR ROYAL HIGHNESS, YOU SEE THE IMPROVEMENTS TO OUR GERMAN-TOMANIAN INDUSTRY SINCE YOU WERE A CHILD HERE, LIKE NUMBER FOUR.
HERR ROTWANG'S TECHNOLOGY CREATED THE MAN-MACHINE MARIA, BUT SHE WAS, PERHAPS, TOO INTELLIGENT. SHE SUBJUGATED THE BERLIN METROPOLIS.
HOWEVER, DR. GOLDFOOT HERE HAS *MODIFIED* THE DESIGN. THESE MODELS, WITH RUDIMENTARY INTELLIGENCE AND GREATER CHEST CAPACITY, ARE FAR MORE POPULAR.
THROUGH OUR U.S. SYMPATHISER GENERAL *MIDWINTER,* WE ARE CURRENTLY EXPORTING THEM TO NORTH AMERICA IN CONSIDERABLE *VOLUME...*

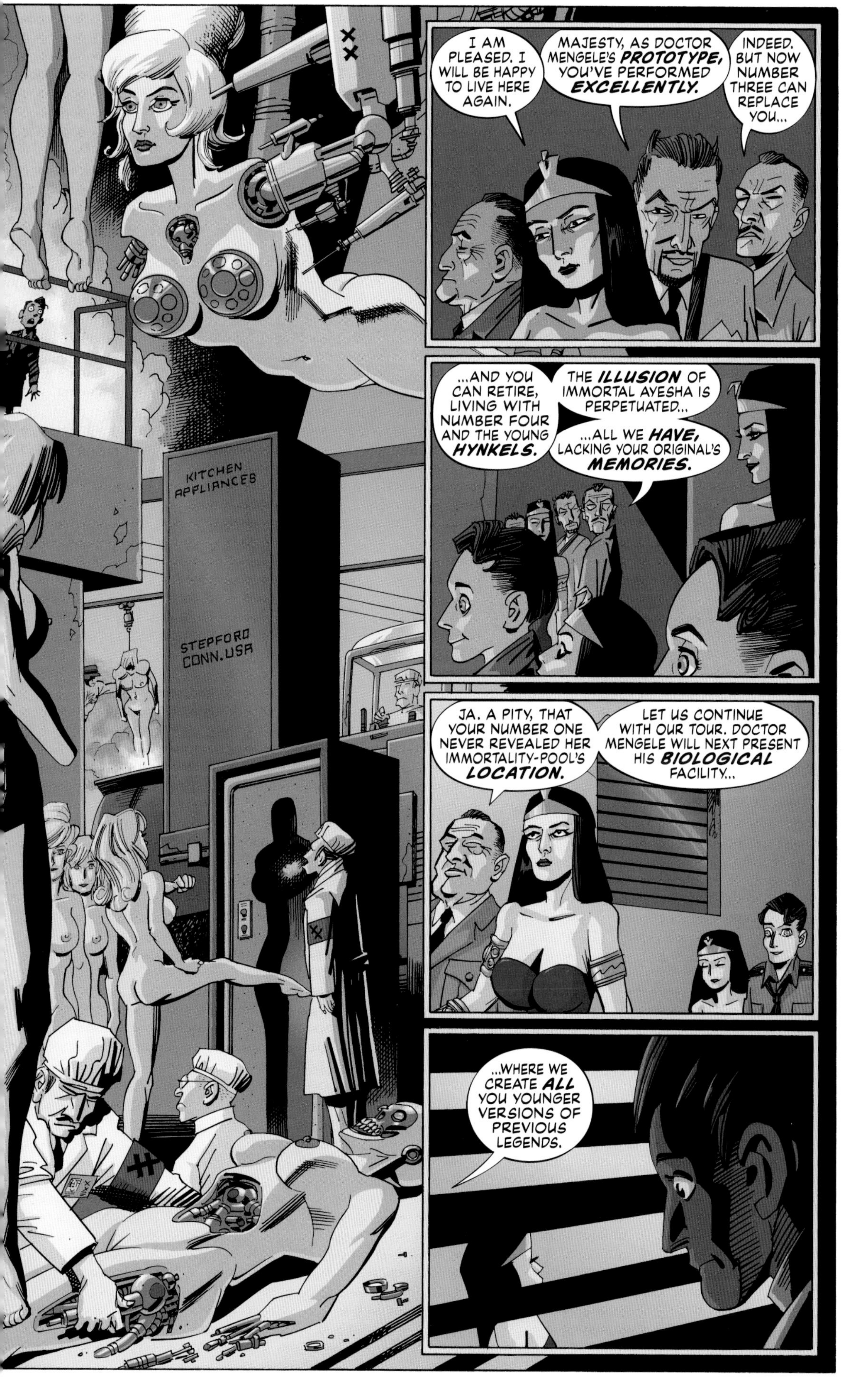
KITCHEN APPLIANCES
STEPFORD CONN. USA
I AM PLEASED. I WILL BE HAPPY TO LIVE HERE AGAIN.
MAJESTY, AS DOCTOR MENGELE'S PROTOTYPE, YOU'VE PERFORMED EXCELLENTLY.
INDEED. BUT NOW NUMBER THREE CAN REPLACE YOU...
...AND YOU CAN RETIRE, LIVING WITH NUMBER FOUR AND THE YOUNG HYNKELS.
THE ILLUSION OF IMMORTAL AYESHA IS PERPETUATED...
...ALL WE HAVE, LACKING YOUR ORIGINAL'S MEMORIES.
JA. A PITY, THAT YOUR NUMBER ONE NEVER REVEALED HER IMMORTALITY-POOL'S LOCATION.
LET US CONTINUE WITH OUR TOUR. DOCTOR MENGELE WILL NEXT PRESENT HIS BIOLOGICAL FACILITY...
...WHERE WE CREATE ALL YOU YOUNGER VERSIONS OF PREVIOUS LEGENDS.

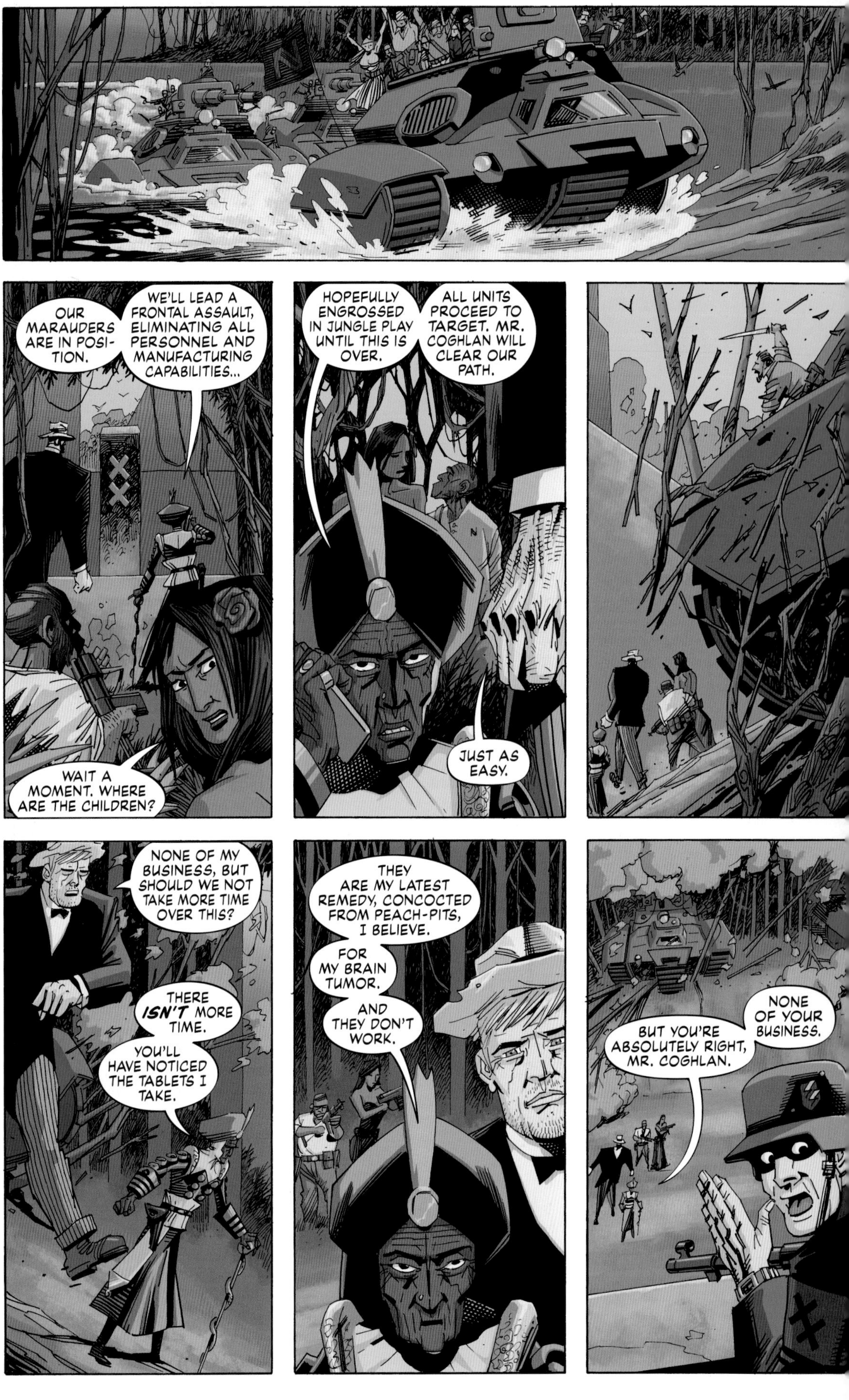

OUR MARAUDERS ARE IN POSITION.
WE'LL LEAD A FRONTAL ASSAULT, ELIMINATING ALL PERSONNEL AND MANUFACTURING CAPABILITIES...
WAIT A MOMENT. WHERE ARE THE CHILDREN?
HOPEFULLY ENGROSSED IN JUNGLE PLAY UNTIL THIS IS OVER.
ALL UNITS PROCEED TO TARGET. MR. COGHLAN WILL CLEAR OUR PATH.
JUST AS EASY.
NONE OF MY BUSINESS, BUT SHOULD WE NOT TAKE MORE TIME OVER THIS?
THERE ***ISN'T*** MORE TIME.
YOU'LL HAVE NOTICED THE TABLETS I TAKE.
THEY ARE MY LATEST REMEDY, CONCOCTED FROM PEACH-PITS, I BELIEVE.
FOR MY BRAIN TUMOR.
AND THEY DON'T WORK.
NONE OF YOUR BUSINESS.
BUT YOU'RE ABSOLUTELY RIGHT, MR. COGHLAN.

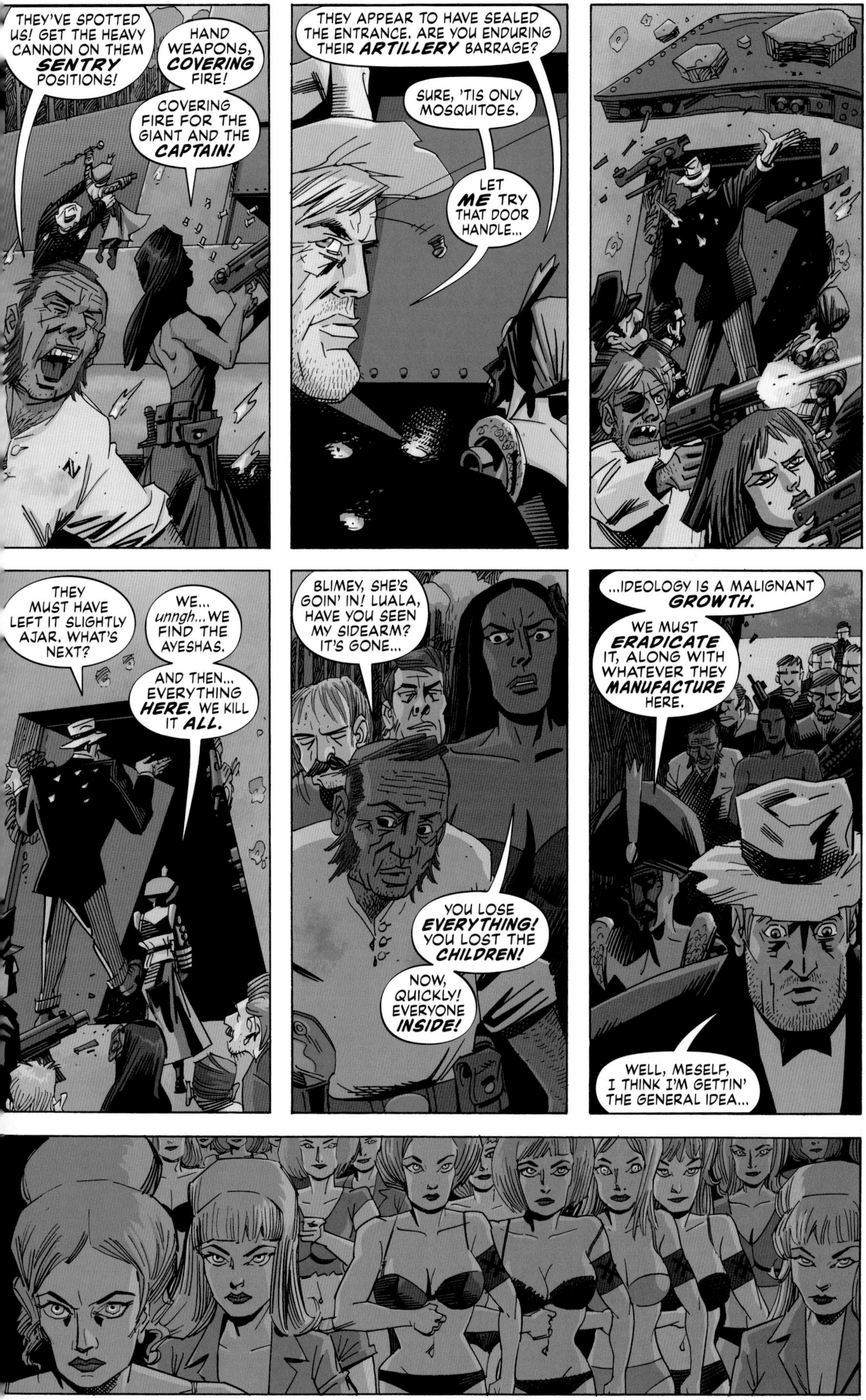

THEY'VE SPOTTED US! GET THE HEAVY CANNON ON THEM SENTRY POSITIONS!
HAND WEAPONS, COVERING FIRE!
COVERING FIRE FOR THE GIANT AND THE CAPTAIN!
THEY APPEAR TO HAVE SEALED THE ENTRANCE. ARE YOU ENDURING THEIR ARTILLERY BARRAGE?
SURE, 'TIS ONLY MOSQUITOES.
LET ME TRY THAT DOOR HANDLE...
THEY MUST HAVE LEFT IT SLIGHTLY AJAR. WHAT'S NEXT?
WE... unngh...WE FIND THE AYESHAS.
AND THEN... EVERYTHING HERE. WE KILL IT ALL.
BLIMEY, SHE'S GOIN' IN! LUALA, HAVE YOU SEEN MY SIDEARM? IT'S GONE...
YOU LOSE EVERYTHING! YOU LOST THE CHILDREN!
NOW, QUICKLY! EVERYONE INSIDE!
...IDEOLOGY IS A MALIGNANT GROWTH.
WE MUST ERADICATE IT, ALONG WITH WHATEVER THEY MANUFACTURE HERE.
WELL, MESELF, I THINK I'M GETTIN' THE GENERAL IDEA...

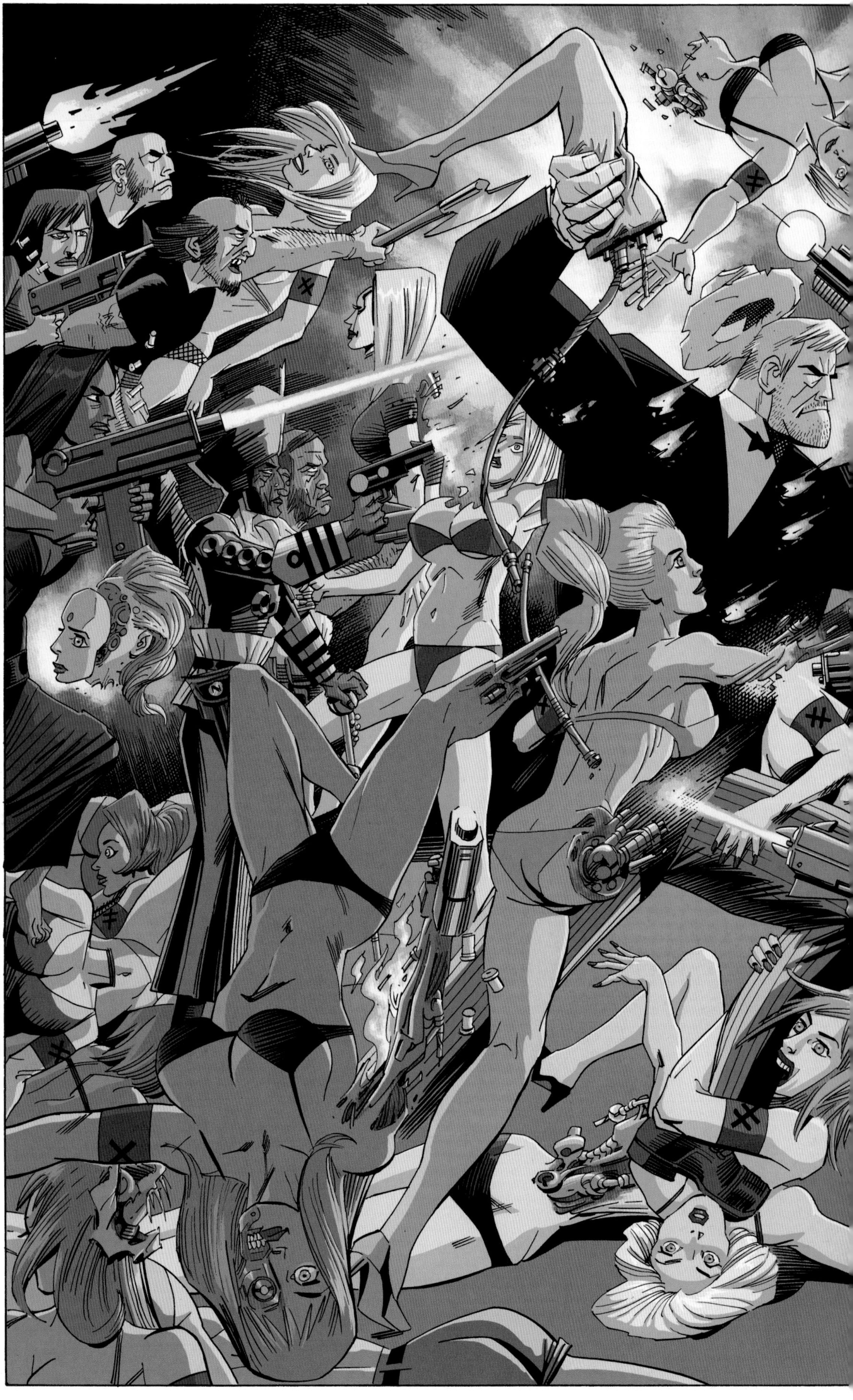

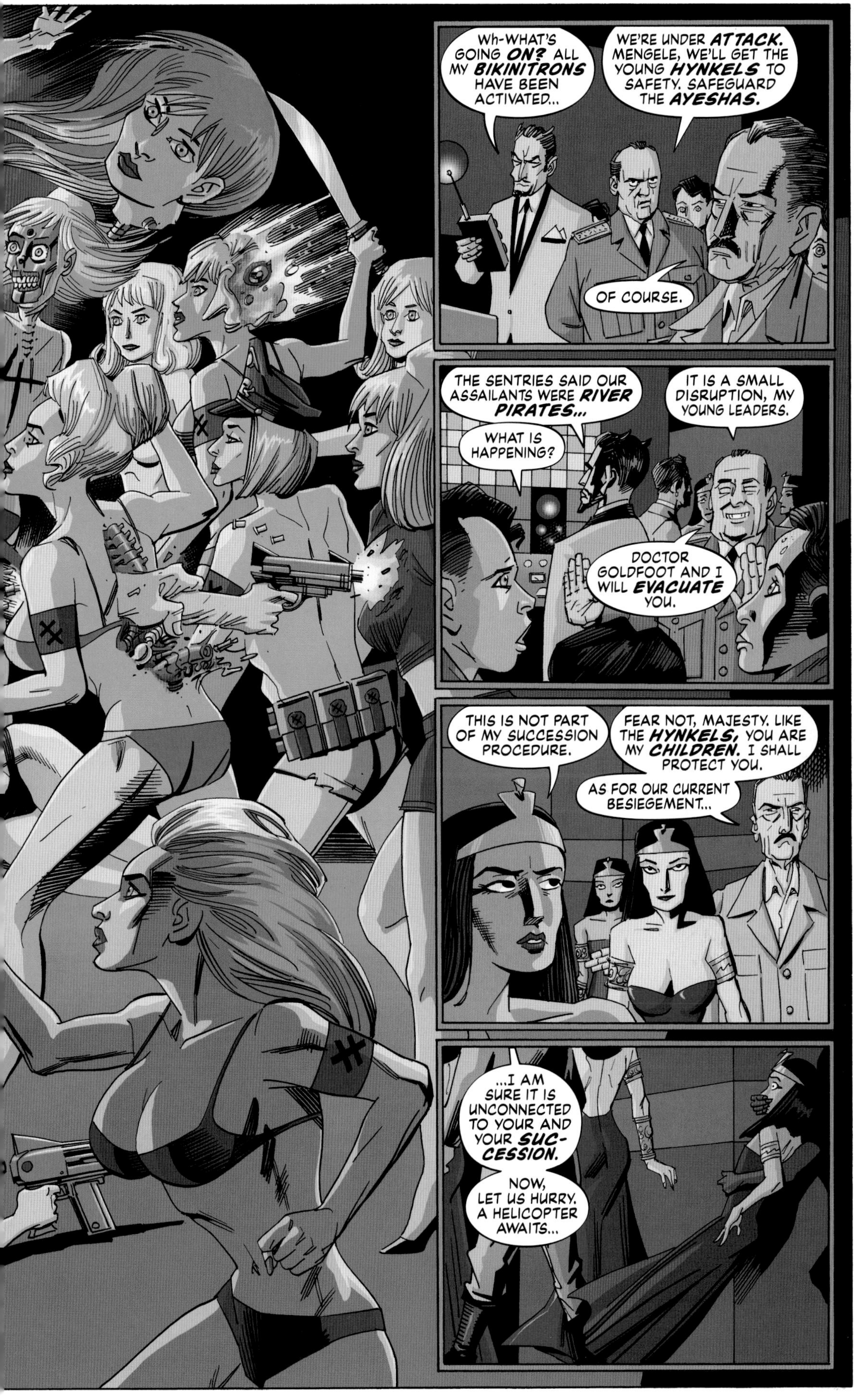

Wh-WHAT'S GOING ON? ALL MY BIKINITRONS HAVE BEEN ACTIVATED...
WE'RE UNDER ATTACK. MENGELE, WE'LL GET THE YOUNG HYNKELS TO SAFETY. SAFEGUARD THE AYESHAS.
OF COURSE.
THE SENTRIES SAID OUR ASSAILANTS WERE RIVER PIRATES...
IT IS A SMALL DISRUPTION, MY YOUNG LEADERS.
WHAT IS HAPPENING?
DOCTOR GOLDFOOT AND I WILL EVACUATE YOU.
THIS IS NOT PART OF MY SUCCESSION PROCEDURE.
FEAR NOT, MAJESTY. LIKE THE HYNKELS, YOU ARE MY CHILDREN. I SHALL PROTECT YOU.
AS FOR OUR CURRENT BESIEGEMENT...
...I AM SURE IT IS UNCONNECTED TO YOUR AND YOUR SUC-CESSION.
NOW, LET US HURRY. A HELICOPTER AWAITS...

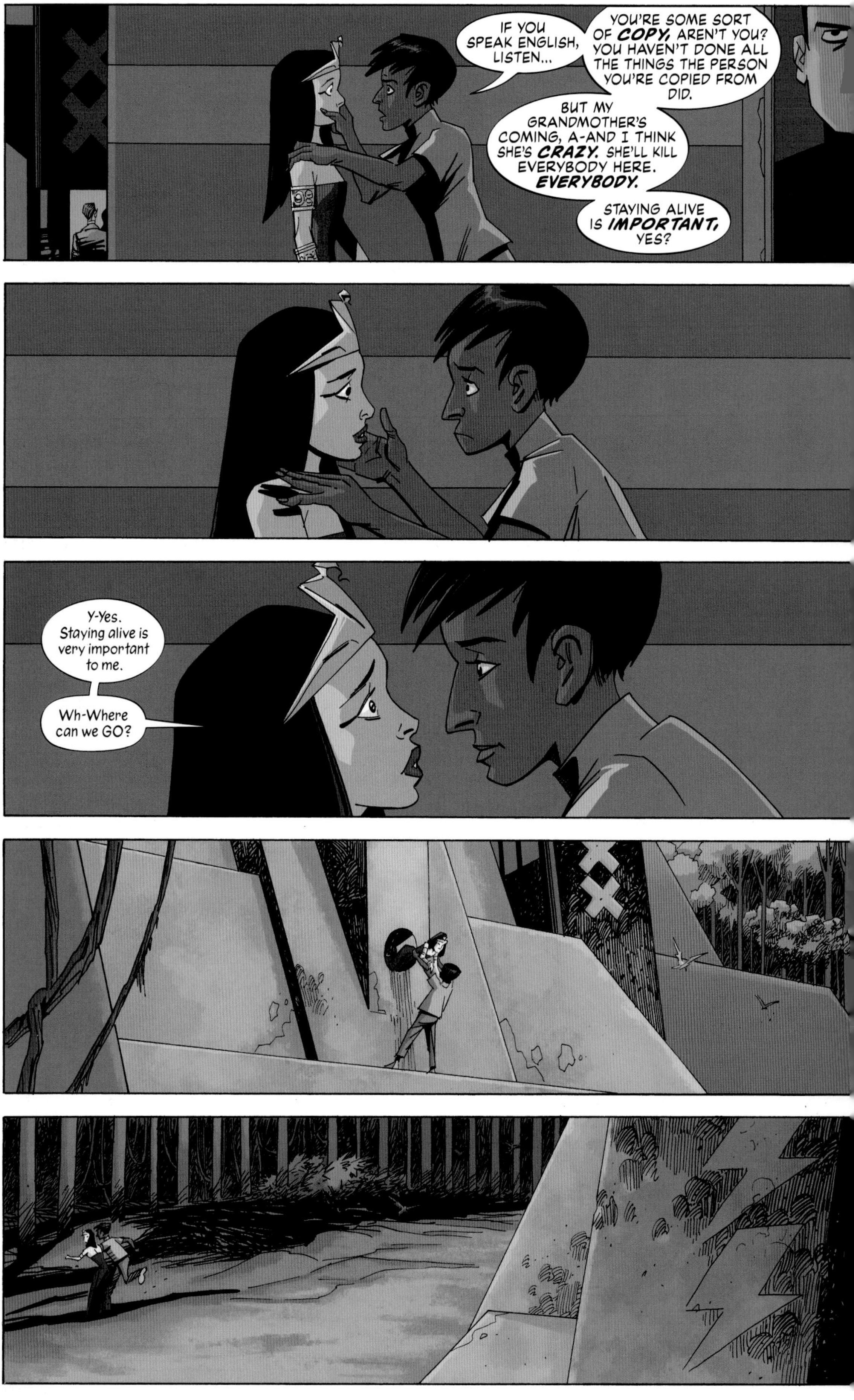
IF YOU SPEAK ENGLISH, LISTEN...
YOU'RE SOME SORT OF COPY, AREN'T YOU? YOU HAVEN'T DONE ALL THE THINGS THE PERSON YOU'RE COPIED FROM DID.
BUT MY GRANDMOTHER'S COMING, A-AND I THINK SHE'S CRAZY. SHE'LL KILL EVERYBODY HERE. EVERYBODY.
STAYING ALIVE IS IMPORTANT, YES?
Y-Yes. Staying alive is very important to me.
Wh-Where can we GO?

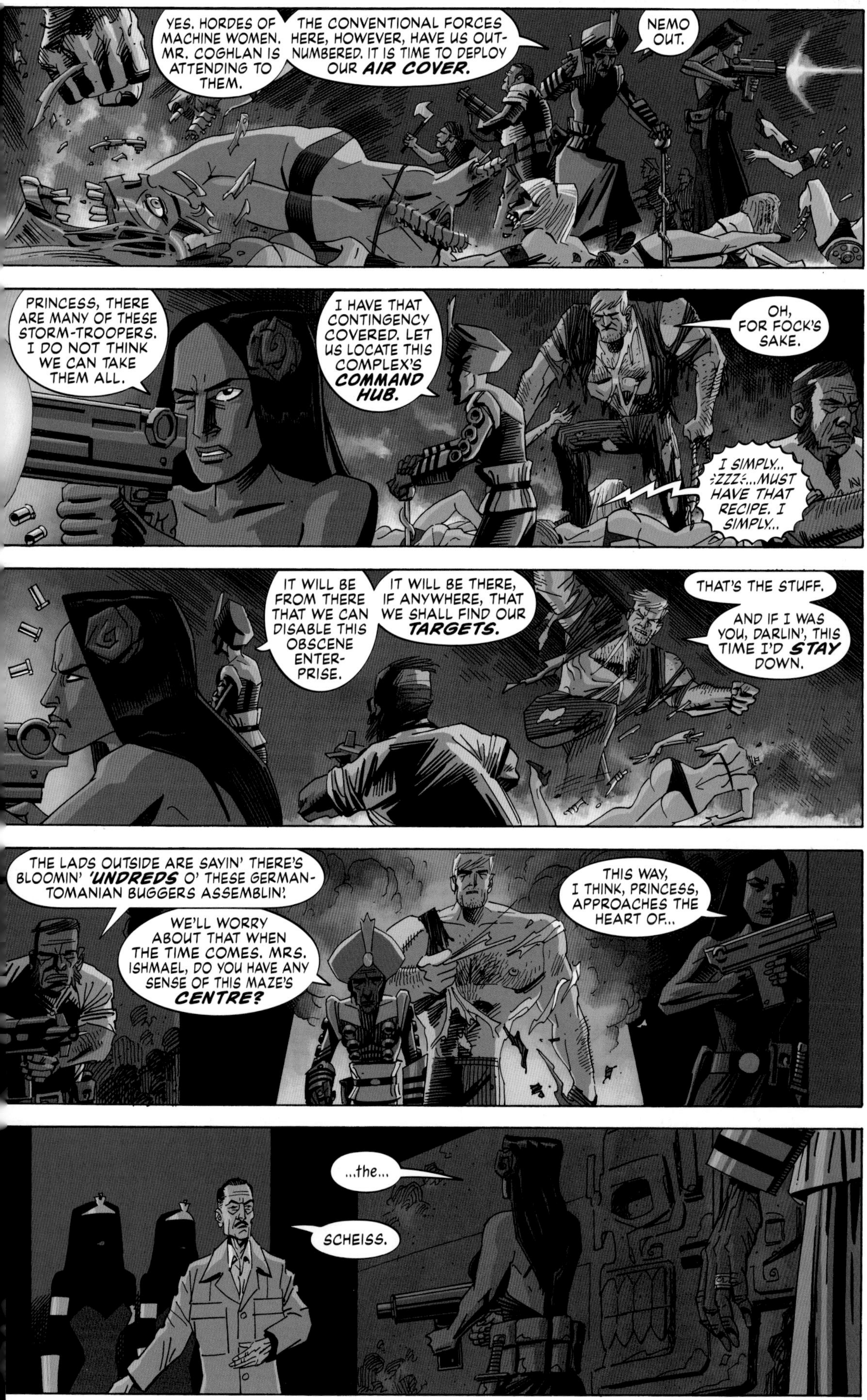
YES. HORDES OF MACHINE WOMEN. MR. COGHLAN IS ATTENDING TO THEM.
THE CONVENTIONAL FORCES HERE, HOWEVER, HAVE US OUT-NUMBERED. IT IS TIME TO DEPLOY OUR AIR COVER.
NEMO OUT.
PRINCESS, THERE ARE MANY OF THESE STORM-TROOPERS. I DO NOT THINK WE CAN TAKE THEM ALL.
I HAVE THAT CONTINGENCY COVERED. LET US LOCATE THIS COMPLEX'S COMMAND HUB.
OH, FOR FOCK'S SAKE.
I SIMPLY... ZZZ...MUST HAVE THAT RECIPE. I SIMPLY...
IT WILL BE FROM THERE THAT WE CAN DISABLE THIS OBSCENE ENTER-PRISE.
IT WILL BE THERE, IF ANYWHERE, THAT WE SHALL FIND OUR TARGETS.
THAT'S THE STUFF.
AND IF I WAS YOU, DARLIN', THIS TIME I'D STAY DOWN.
THE LADS OUTSIDE ARE SAYIN' THERE'S BLOOMIN' 'UNDREDS O' THESE GERMAN-TOMANIAN BUGGERS ASSEMBLIN'.
WE'LL WORRY ABOUT THAT WHEN THE TIME COMES. MRS. ISHMAEL, DO YOU HAVE ANY SENSE OF THIS MAZE'S CENTRE?
THIS WAY, I THINK, PRINCESS, APPROACHES THE HEART OF...
...the...
SCHEISS.

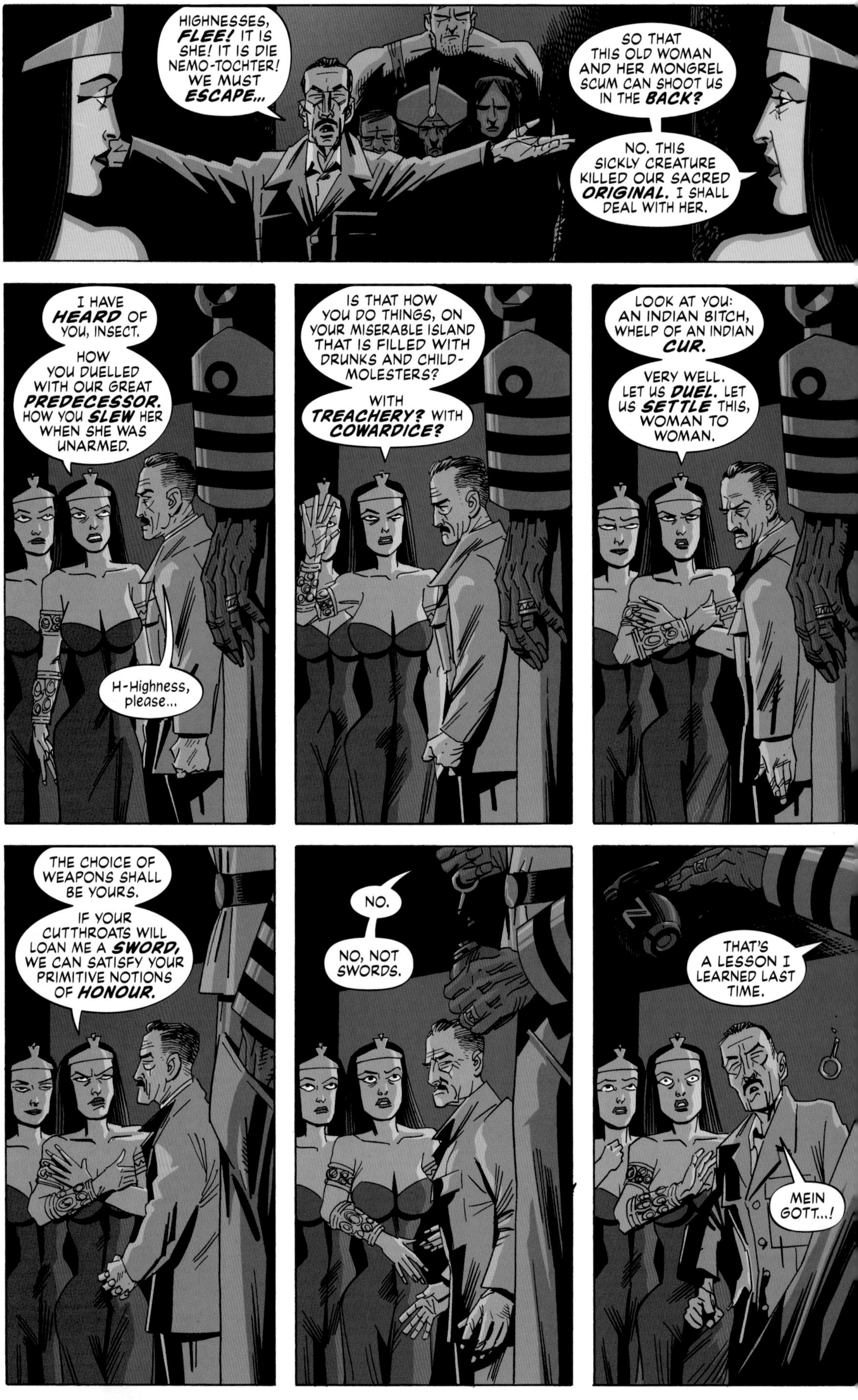
HIGHNESSES, FLEE! IT IS SHE! IT IS DIE NEMO-TOCHTER! WE MUST ESCAPE...
SO THAT THIS OLD WOMAN AND HER MONGREL SCUM CAN SHOOT US IN THE BACK?
NO. THIS SICKLY CREATURE KILLED OUR SACRED ORIGINAL. I SHALL DEAL WITH HER.
I HAVE HEARD OF YOU, INSECT.
HOW YOU DUELLED WITH OUR GREAT PREDECESSOR. HOW YOU SLEW HER WHEN SHE WAS UNARMED.
H-Highness, please...
IS THAT HOW YOU DO THINGS, ON YOUR MISERABLE ISLAND THAT IS FILLED WITH DRUNKS AND CHILD-MOLESTERS?
WITH TREACHERY? WITH COWARDICE?
LOOK AT YOU: AN INDIAN BITCH, WHELP OF AN INDIAN CUR.
VERY WELL. LET US DUEL. LET US SETTLE THIS, WOMAN TO WOMAN.
THE CHOICE OF WEAPONS SHALL BE YOURS.
IF YOUR CUTTHROATS WILL LOAN ME A SWORD, WE CAN SATISFY YOUR PRIMITIVE NOTIONS OF HONOUR.
NO.
NO, NOT SWORDS.
THAT'S A LESSON I LEARNED LAST TIME.
MEIN GOTT...!

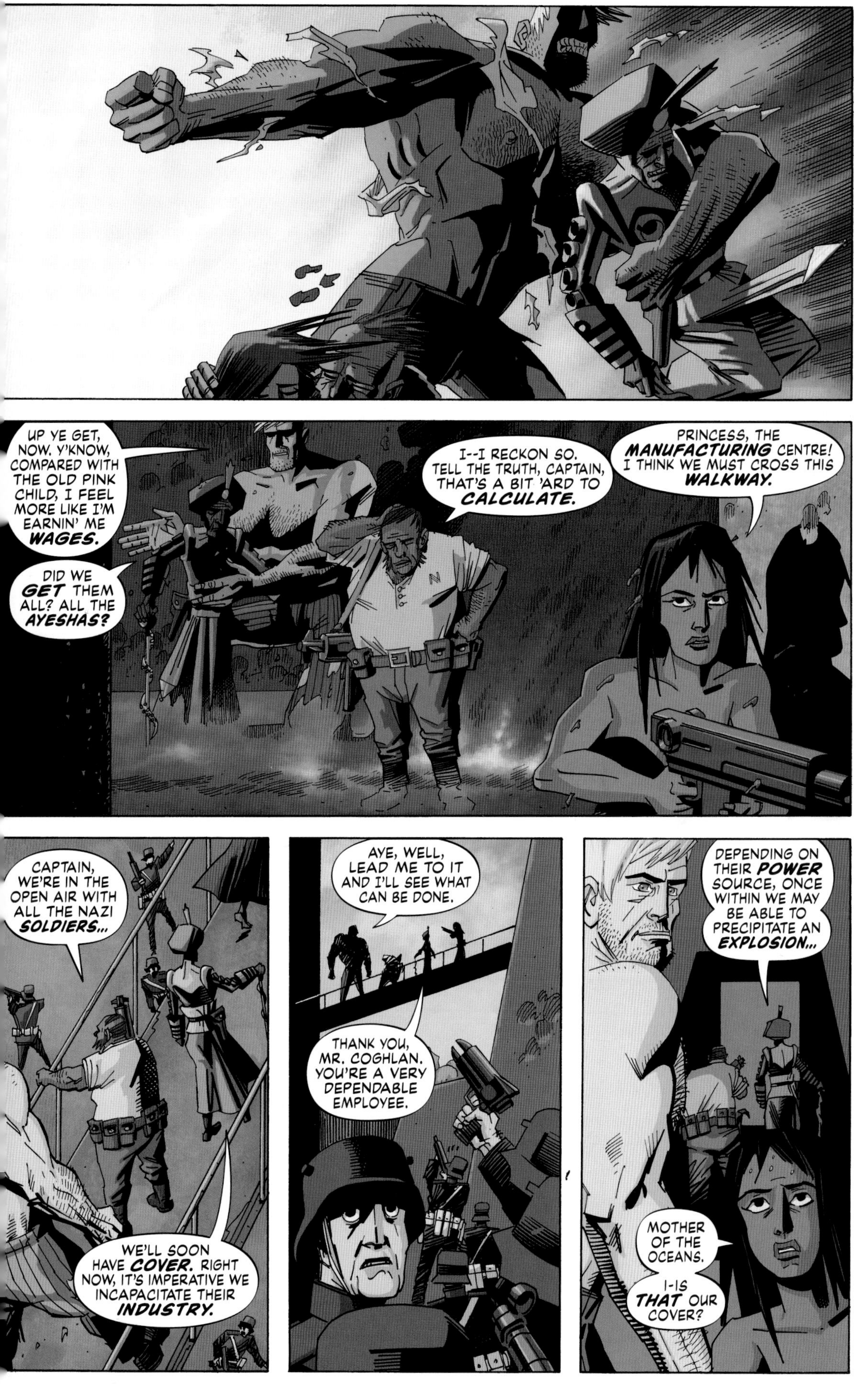
UP YE GET, NOW. Y'KNOW, COMPARED WITH THE OLD PINK CHILD, I FEEL MORE LIKE I'M EARNIN' ME WAGES.
DID WE GET THEM ALL? ALL THE AYESHAS?
I--I RECKON SO. TELL THE TRUTH, CAPTAIN, THAT'S A BIT 'ARD TO CALCULATE.
PRINCESS, THE MANUFACTURING CENTRE! I THINK WE MUST CROSS THIS WALKWAY.
CAPTAIN, WE'RE IN THE OPEN AIR WITH ALL THE NAZI SOLDIERS...
WE'LL SOON HAVE COVER. RIGHT NOW, IT'S IMPERATIVE WE INCAPACITATE THEIR INDUSTRY.
AYE, WELL, LEAD ME TO IT AND I'LL SEE WHAT CAN BE DONE.
THANK YOU, MR. COGHLAN. YOU'RE A VERY DEPENDABLE EMPLOYEE.
DEPENDING ON THEIR POWER SOURCE, ONCE WITHIN WE MAY BE ABLE TO PRECIPITATE AN EXPLOSION...
MOTHER OF THE OCEANS.
I-IS THAT OUR COVER?

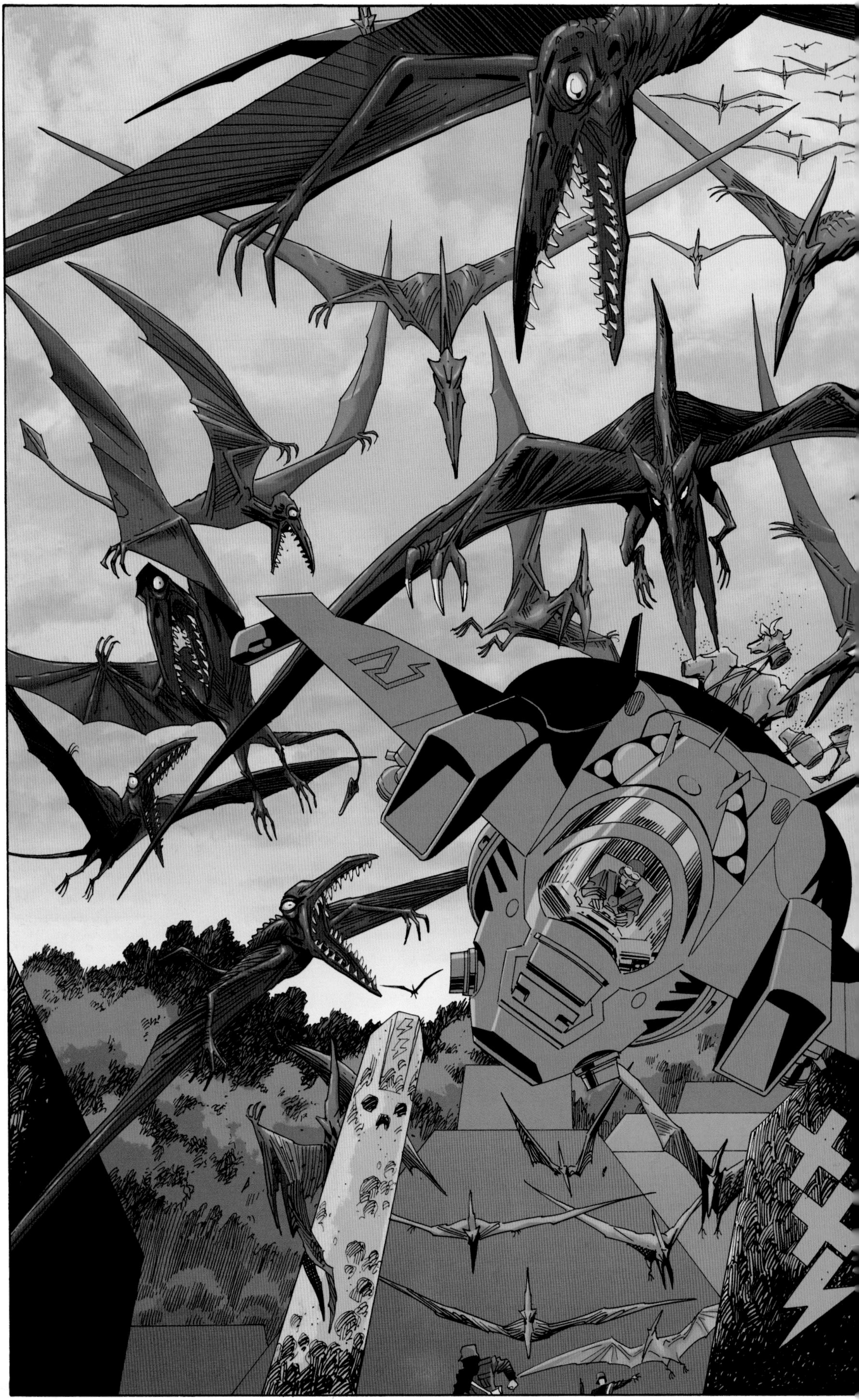

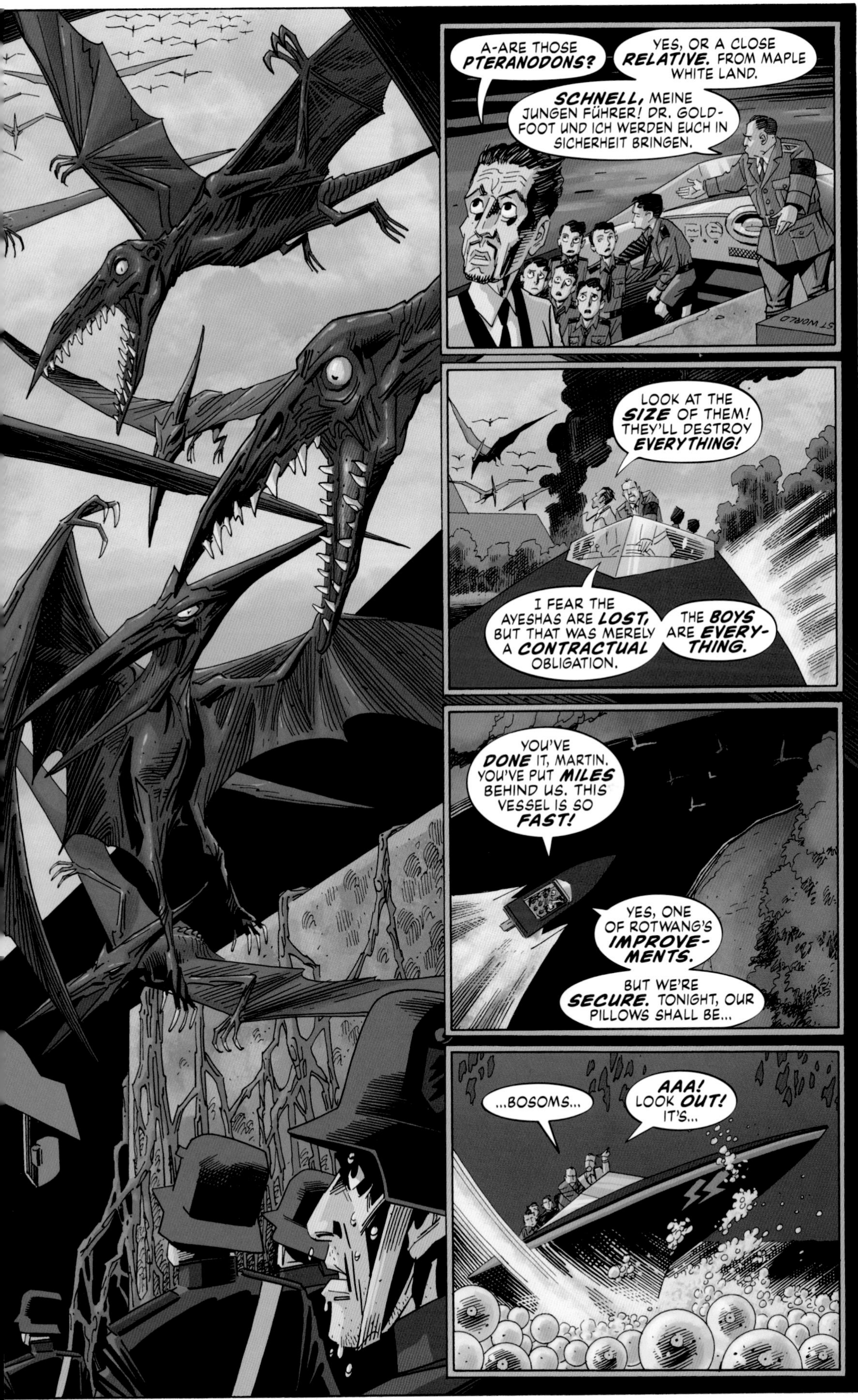
A-ARE THOSE PTERANODONS?
YES, OR A CLOSE RELATIVE. FROM MAPLE WHITE LAND.
SCHNELL, MEINE JUNGEN FÜHRER! DR. GOLDFOOT UND ICH WERDEN EUCH IN SICHERHEIT BRINGEN.
LOOK AT THE SIZE OF THEM! THEY'LL DESTROY EVERYTHING!
I FEAR THE AYESHAS ARE LOST, BUT THAT WAS MERELY A CONTRACTUAL OBLIGATION.
THE BOYS ARE EVERYTHING.
YOU'VE DONE IT, MARTIN. YOU'VE PUT MILES BEHIND US. THIS VESSEL IS SO FAST!
YES, ONE OF ROTWANG'S IMPROVEMENTS.
BUT WE'RE SECURE. TONIGHT, OUR PILLOWS SHALL BE...
...BOSOMS...
AAA! LOOK OUT! IT'S...

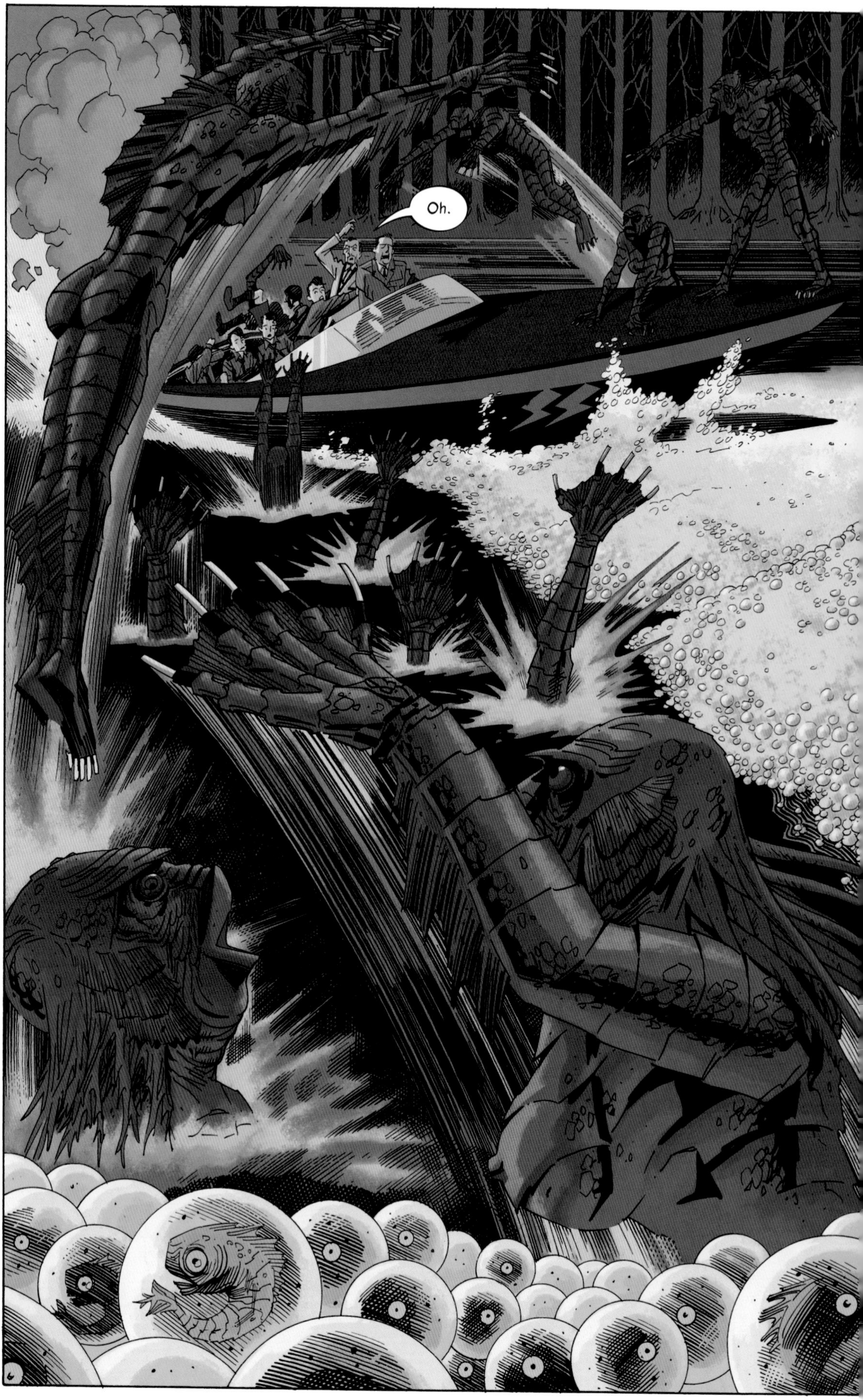
Oh.

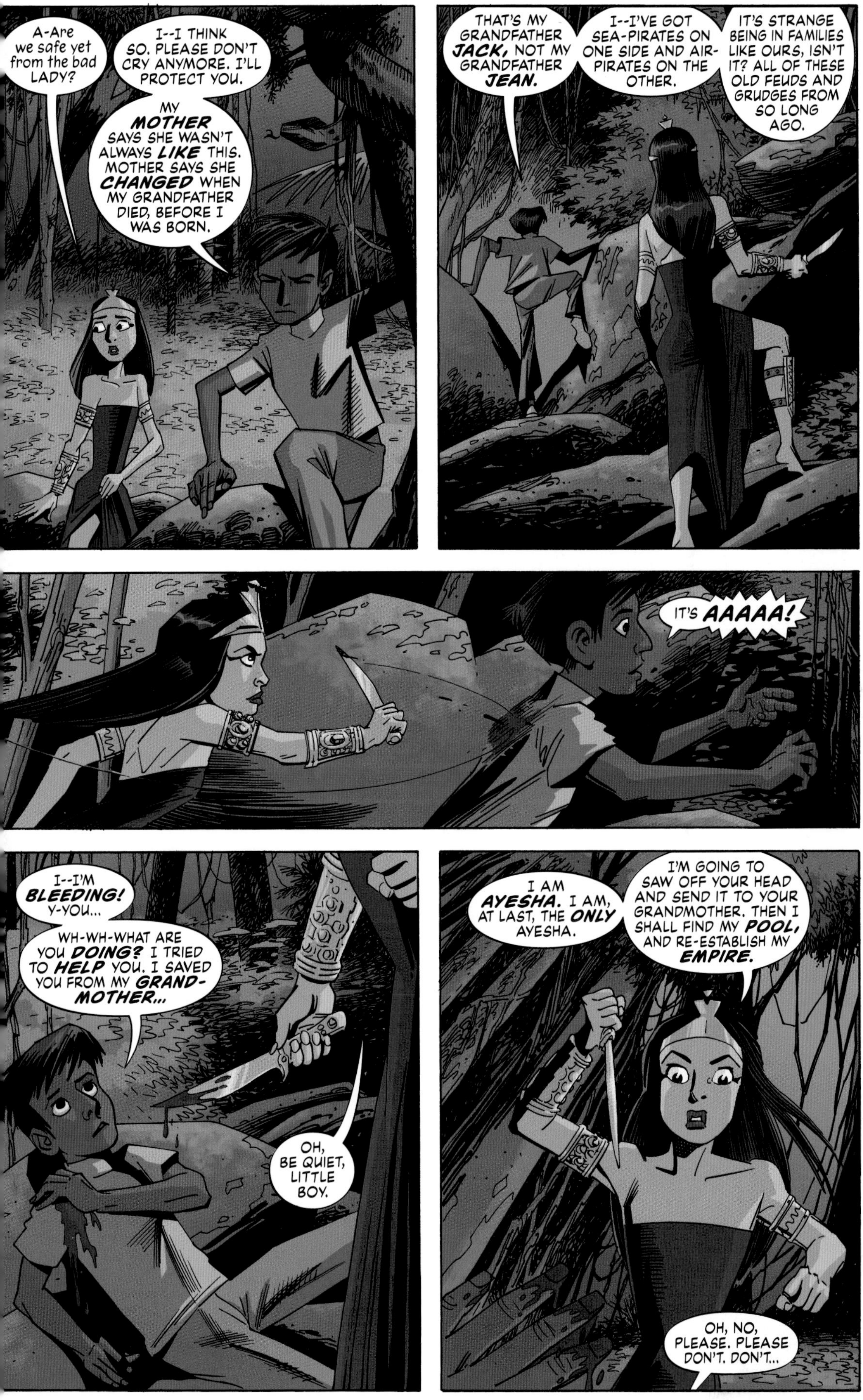
A-Are we safe yet from the bad LADY?
I--I THINK SO. PLEASE DON'T CRY ANYMORE. I'LL PROTECT YOU.
MY MOTHER SAYS SHE WASN'T ALWAYS LIKE THIS. MOTHER SAYS SHE CHANGED WHEN MY GRANDFATHER DIED, BEFORE I WAS BORN.
THAT'S MY GRANDFATHER JACK, NOT MY GRANDFATHER JEAN.
I--I'VE GOT SEA-PIRATES ON ONE SIDE AND AIR-PIRATES ON THE OTHER.
IT'S STRANGE BEING IN FAMILIES LIKE OURS, ISN'T IT? ALL OF THESE OLD FEUDS AND GRUDGES FROM SO LONG AGO.
IT'S AAAAA!
I--I'M BLEEDING! Y-YOU...
WH-WH-WHAT ARE YOU DOING? I TRIED TO HELP YOU. I SAVED YOU FROM MY GRAND-MOTHER...
OH, BE QUIET, LITTLE BOY.
I AM AYESHA. I AM, AT LAST, THE ONLY AYESHA.
I'M GOING TO SAW OFF YOUR HEAD AND SEND IT TO YOUR GRANDMOTHER. THEN I SHALL FIND MY POOL, AND RE-ESTABLISH MY EMPIRE.
OH, NO, PLEASE. PLEASE DON'T. DON'T...

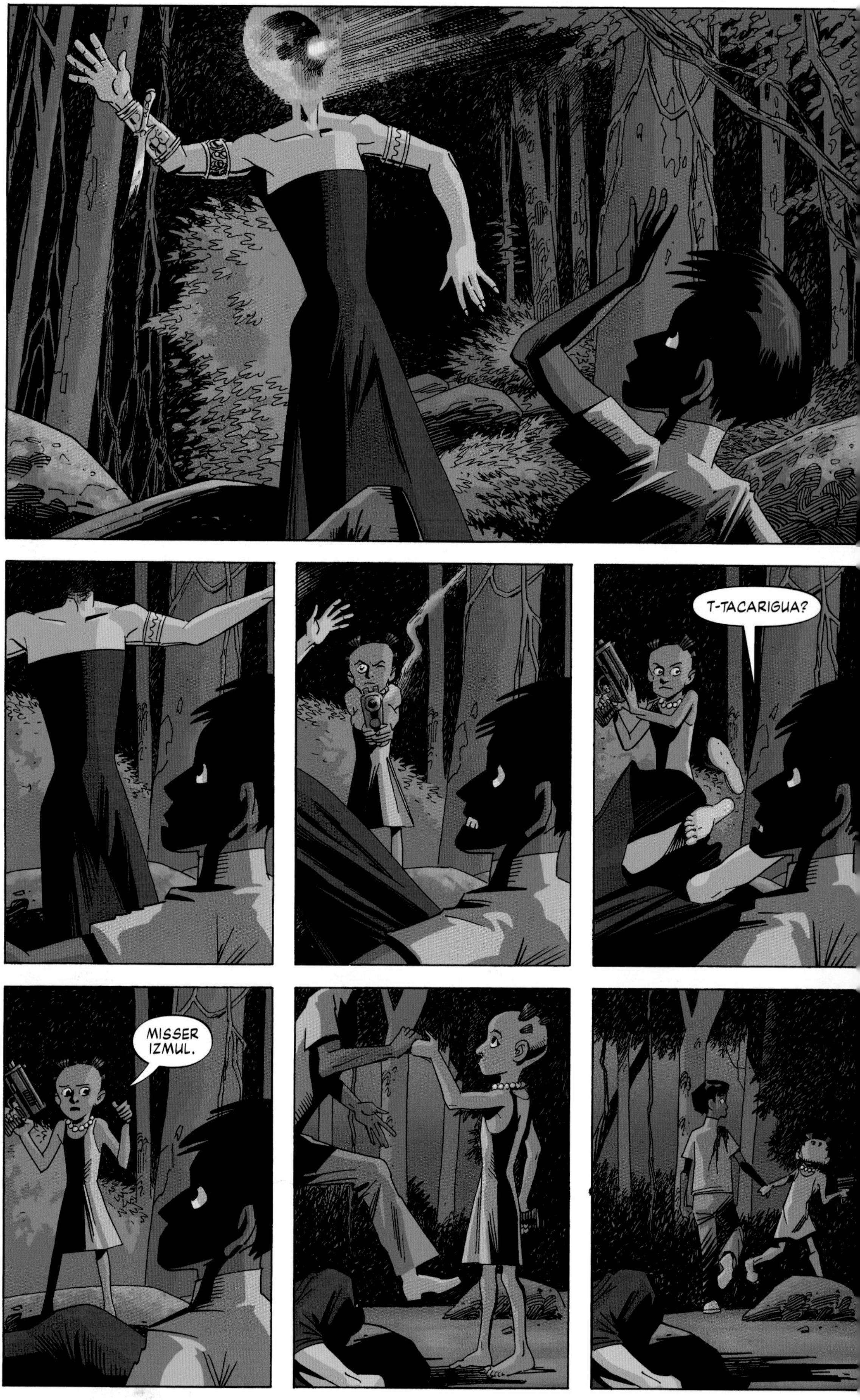
T-TACARIGUA?
MISSER IZMUL.

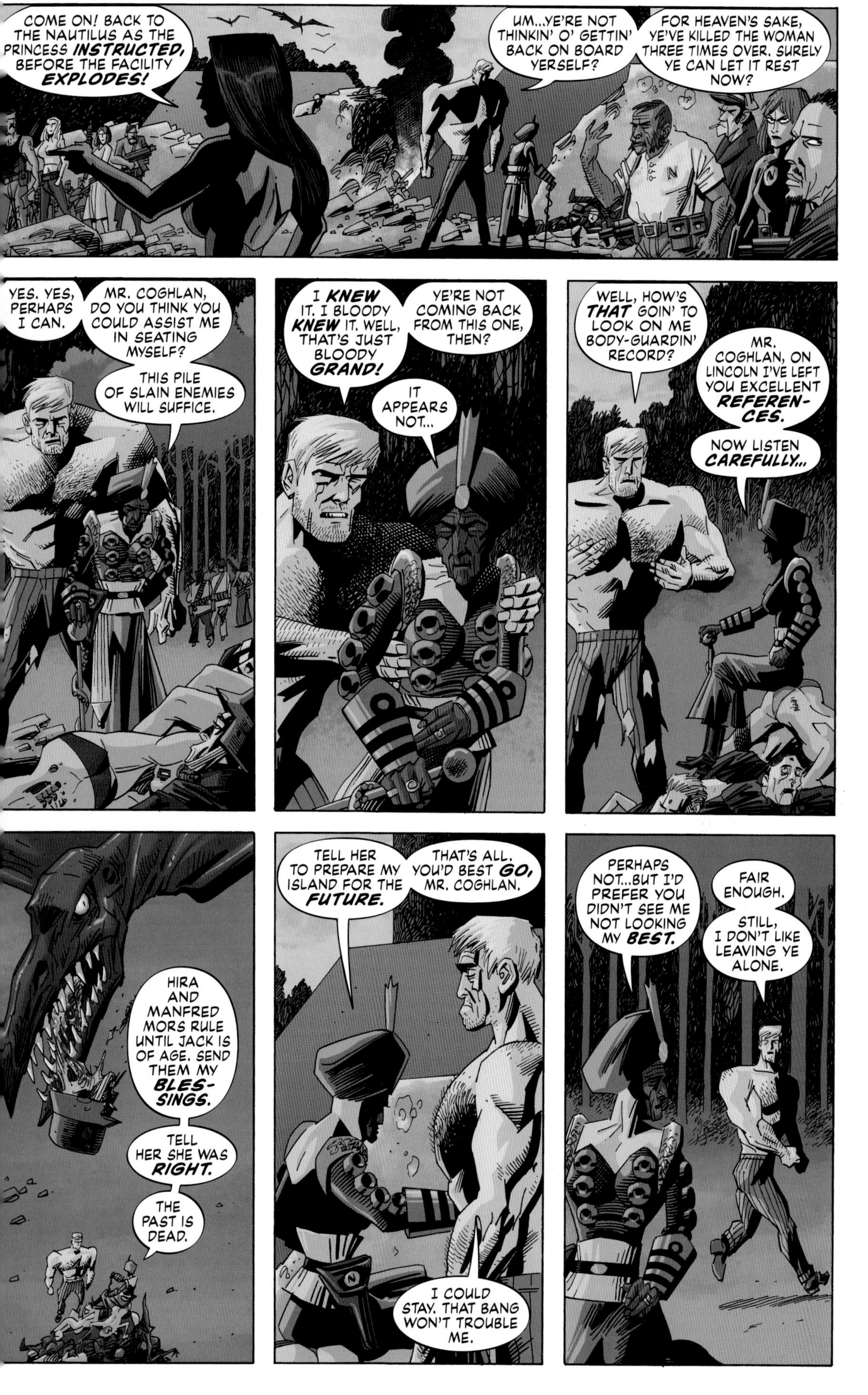

COME ON! BACK TO THE NAUTILUS AS THE PRINCESS INSTRUCTED, BEFORE THE FACILITY EXPLODES!
UM...YE'RE NOT THINKIN' O' GETTIN' BACK ON BOARD YERSELF?
FOR HEAVEN'S SAKE, YE'VE KILLED THE WOMAN THREE TIMES OVER. SURELY YE CAN LET IT REST NOW?
YES. YES, PERHAPS I CAN.
MR. COGHLAN, DO YOU THINK YOU COULD ASSIST ME IN SEATING MYSELF?
THIS PILE OF SLAIN ENEMIES WILL SUFFICE.
I KNEW IT. I BLOODY KNEW IT. WELL, THAT'S JUST BLOODY GRAND!
YE'RE NOT COMING BACK FROM THIS ONE, THEN?
IT APPEARS NOT...
WELL, HOW'S THAT GOIN' TO LOOK ON ME BODY-GUARDIN' RECORD?
MR. COGHLAN, ON LINCOLN I'VE LEFT YOU EXCELLENT REFEREN-CES.
NOW LISTEN CAREFULLY...
HIRA AND MANFRED MORS RULE UNTIL JACK IS OF AGE. SEND THEM MY BLES-SINGS.
TELL HER SHE WAS RIGHT.
THE PAST IS DEAD.
TELL HER TO PREPARE MY ISLAND FOR THE FUTURE.
THAT'S ALL. YOU'D BEST GO, MR. COGHLAN.
I COULD STAY. THAT BANG WON'T TROUBLE ME.
PERHAPS NOT...BUT I'D PREFER YOU DIDN'T SEE ME NOT LOOKING MY BEST.
FAIR ENOUGH.
STILL, I DON'T LIKE LEAVING YE ALONE.

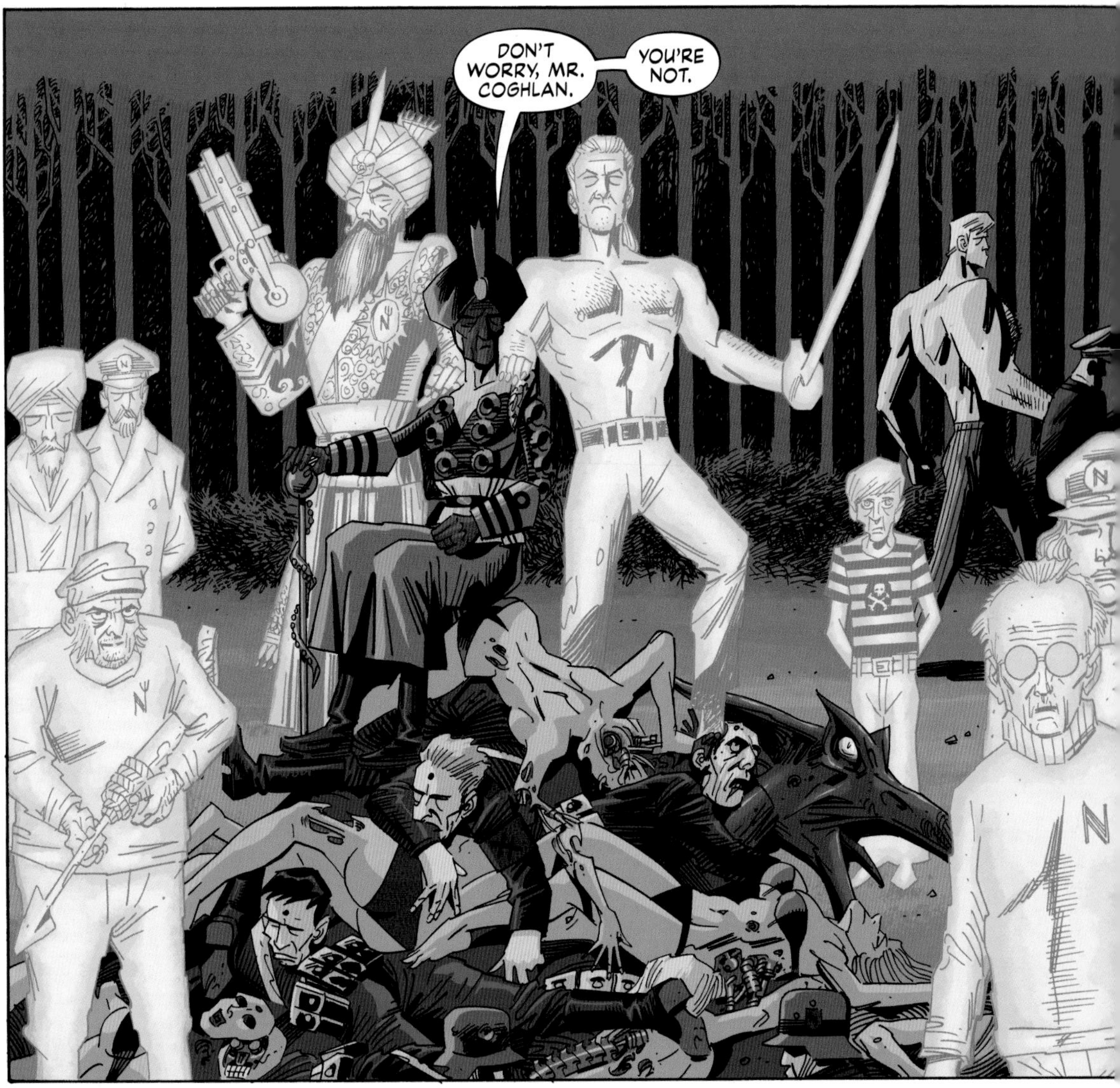
DON'T WORRY, MR. COGHLAN.
YOU'RE NOT.

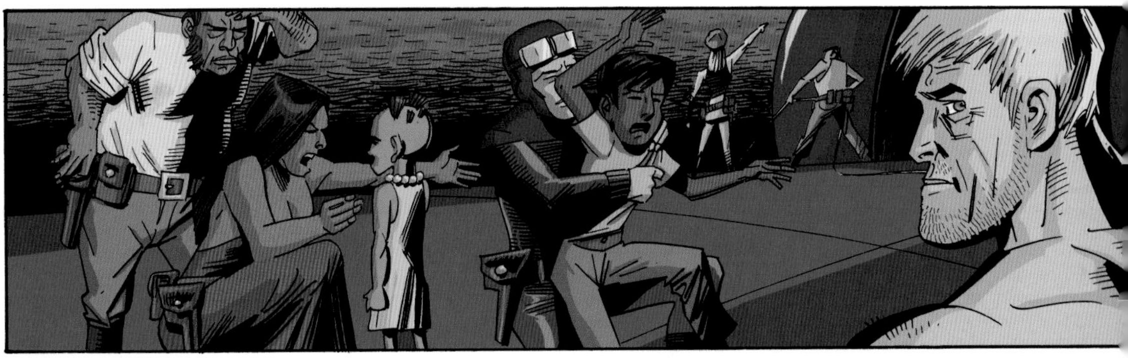

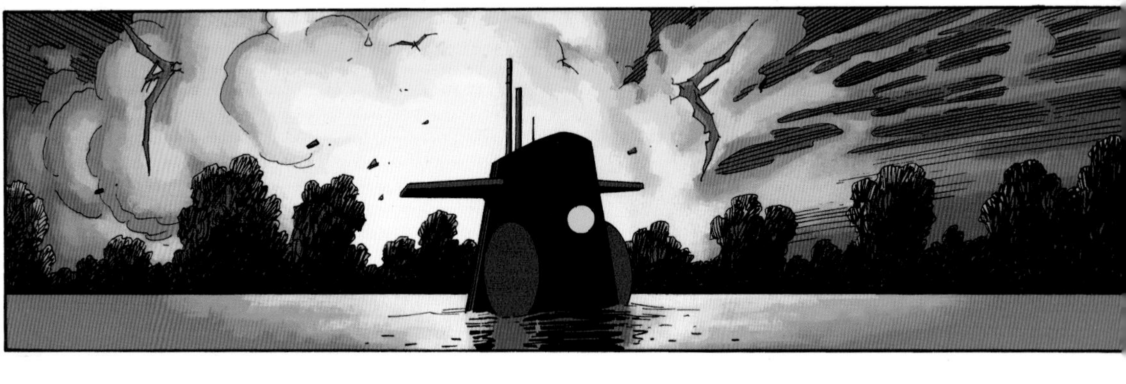

Lincoln Island, 1987.

ACH, HERR KAPITÄN. IT IS GOOD TO SEE SO MANY OF THE WORLD'S GREAT VILLAINS PRESENT HERE FOR THIS *UNVEILING.*

THANK YOU, HELMUT. I AM SORRY THAT YOUR MOTHER, FRAU MABUSE, COULD NOT BE HERE.

PLEASE SEND HER MY WISHES FOR A SWIFT *RECOVERY.*

YOU ARE TOO *CLOSE!* KEEP *BACK* FROM HIM, OR THIS WILL NOT BE *FUNNY.*

¿ULK?

THANK YOU, MR. ISHMAEL, BUT THIS IS A DAY OF *CELEBRATION.* IF PERHAPS WE COULD KEEP THE CASUALTIES TO A BARE *MINIMUM...?*

JACK, *THERE* YOU ARE! THE GENERAL AND I WERE WONDERING IF WE'D BE FORCED TO LAUNCH THE CEREMONY *OURSELVES.*

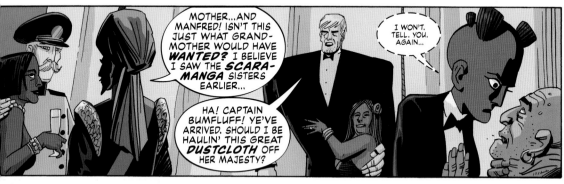

MOTHER...AND MANFRED! ISN'T THIS JUST WHAT GRANDMOTHER WOULD HAVE *WANTED?* I BELIEVE I SAW THE *SCARAMANGA* SISTERS EARLIER...

HA! CAPTAIN BUMFLUFF! YE'VE ARRIVED. SHOULD I BE HAULIN' THIS GREAT *DUSTCLOTH* OFF HER MAJESTY?

I WON'T. TELL. YOU. AGAIN...

AS EVER, MR. COGHLAN, YOU ANTICIPATE MY WISHES.

AND *LUALA.* KNOW THAT I BURNED INCENSE YESTERDAY, ON THE THIRD ANNIVERSARY OF TOBIAS'S *DEMISE.*

IT *WAS?*

RIGHT, NOW, LET'S BE SEEIN' IF I'VE GOT THE MEASURE O' THIS DAMNABLE CONTRAPTION.

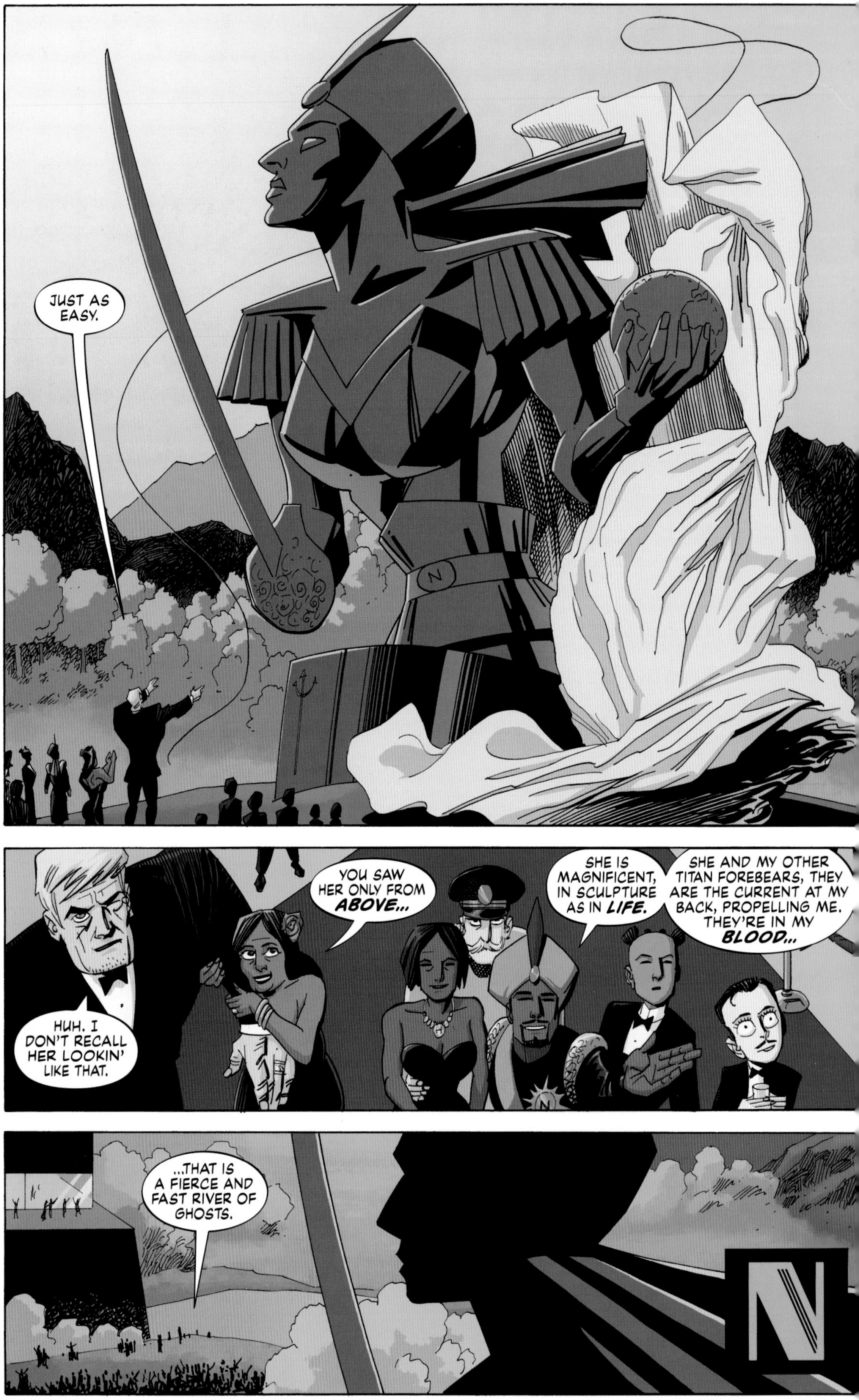
JUST AS EASY.
HUH. I DON'T RECALL HER LOOKIN' LIKE THAT.
YOU SAW HER ONLY FROM *ABOVE...*
SHE IS MAGNIFICENT, IN SCULPTURE AS IN *LIFE.*
SHE AND MY OTHER TITAN FOREBEARS, THEY ARE THE CURRENT AT MY BACK, PROPELLING ME. THEY'RE IN MY *BLOOD...*
...THAT IS A FIERCE AND FAST RIVER OF GHOSTS.

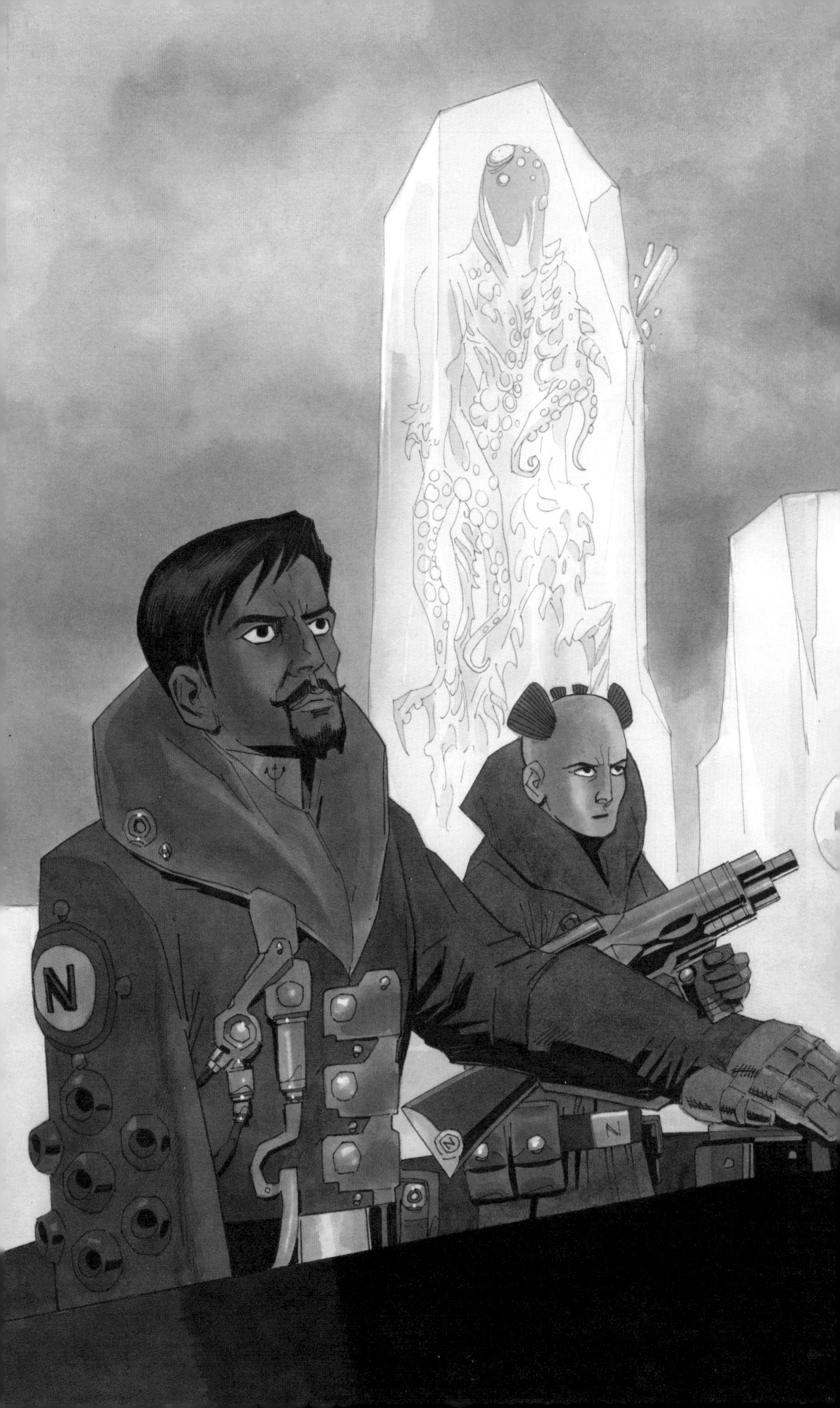